Signature Tastes
of
NEW ORLEANS

"THE UNION MUST
AND
SHALL BE PRESERVED"

SMOKE ALARM

MEDIA

D1709631

Paula's Thanks: To Steven Siler...Thanks for bringing me along for this amazing ride. Thanks for trusting me with your vision and thanks for giving me the best job in the world.

To Rick Walker... Eight years ago you introduced me to New Orleans in your own special way. From the first day I knew I was home.

To Kristen Garriott...my music lovin', bead catchin', foodie daughter who is always looking for an excuse to go to New Orleans.

To Cindy Welch...my BFF who taught me the finer art of "Step and Go" and loves Mardi Gras as much as I do.

To my New Orleans family... Ainsley, Amanda, Ann, Caroline, Cherie, Evangeline, Greg, Karla, Lena, Matty, Musa, Pat, Peter, Rick, Tim and Veda ...You make New Orleans home.

And my forever thanks goes to Stan Allsberry... Your help and steadfast love has been invaluable this year. Don't know what I'd do without you.

To the New Orleans restaurants and the foodies that love them... One of the hardest things I had to do was to choose what recipes to include in this book. Many of my favorites are here, but some are not.

Recipes were supplied by the restaurants or listed below: abita.com, www.amanonola.com, www.abita.com, www.americascuisine.com, www.arnaudsrestaurant.com, Bayona, www.blogs.laweekly.com, www.brennansneworleans.com, www.cafedegas.com, www.cdn2-b.examiner.com, www.classiccitybrew.com, www.colorfulplaces.com, community.kingarthurflour.com, Corporate Realty, countryroadsmagazine.com, www.crescentcityfarmersmarket.com, www.deanies.com, easteuropeanfood.about.com, edenaromata.com, www.epicurious.com, www.examiner.com, www.food.com, www.foodandwine.com, www.foodnetwork.com, forums.neworleans.com, www.fox8live.com, www.galatoires.com, www.gulfcoastrecipes.com, www.gumboshop.com, www.jamesbeard.org, www.labocasteaks.com, lxsurvexperience.com, www.middlebarla.com, www.mothersrestaurant.net, www.mrbsbistro.com, www.napoleonhouse.com, neworleansgourmet.tv, www.neworleansrestaurants.com, www.nightclub.com, Old New Orleans Rum, Pat Kahn, www.perfect1864.com, www.plateonline.com, www.projectnola.com, www.recipes.totaldream.org, reconcileneworleans.org, www.ritzcarlton.com, Royal Sonesta Hotel, www.saveur.com, www.savorytv.com, shop.cafedumonde.com, www.starchefs.com, www.tastebook.com, www.tastingtable.com, www.virtualcities.com, www.youtube.com

Welcome to New Orleans information from the following: The Historic New Orleans Collection, www.FrenchQuarter.com, Hungry Town by Tom Fitzmorris

To others unnamed: Because my memory is as long as my hair

Layout by Steven W. Siler

Photo editing by Richard Walker

All photos common license unless otherwise noted.

Photos of 5 Fifty 5, Cafe Du Monde, Commander's Palace, Grand Isle Restaurant, Irvin Mayfield's Jazz Playhouse, Mr. B's Bistro and Red Fish Grill by Paula Garriott

Photo of Acme Oyster House by Beth Jarosz

Photo of Antoine's Restaurant by takethoufood.com

Photo of Bougainvillea House by Pat Kahn

Photo of Bourbon House by Sean Park, takethougood.com

Photo of Cochon Restaurant by Chris Carriero, www.ikangaroo.com

Photo of Feelings Cafe by Marc Kjerland

Photos of a Mano and Casamento's Restaurant by RL Reeves Jr., www.chowpapi.com

Photos of Bistro Daisy, Café Degas, The Delachaise, Emeril's New Orleans, Il Posto Cafe, Iris, The Joint, la Madeleine, Martinique Bistro, Maximo's Italian Grill, MiLa, Muriel's Jackson Square and Sucré by Foodographer.net

Photos of Clancy's Restaurant, La Petite Grocery Restaurant and Bar, Mahony's Po-Boy Shop, and Patois by www.fleurdelicious.com

Photos of: 7 on Fulton by frenchquarterwedding.com Abita Brew Pub by hoiststhemainales.blogspot.com, Angelo Brocato's Italian Ice Cream and Italian Desserts, and Cure by trevsbistro.wordpress.com, Atchafalaya Restaurant by ct-cj.com, Bar Tonique by nolafreepress.com, Bayona by zebraprikket.dk, Bennachin Restaurant by elysasmusingsfromgraceland.blogspot.com, Besh Steakhouse at Harrah's Casino by targetvacations.ca, Bon Ton Café by neworleans.com, Café Amelie by twogirlsturningthirty.wordpress.com, The Camilla Grill by off-myplate.blogspot.com, Central Grocery Co. by lostnewyorkcity.blogspot.com, Coop's Place by thechocolateofmeats.com, Coquette Bistro Wine Bar by ocrewind.blogspot.com, Court of Two Sisters by futuregringo.com, Crescent City Brew House by thebeertraveller.com, Crescent City Pie and Sausage Company by nativepalate.blogspot.com, Dat Dog by poboylivinrich.com, Deanie's Seafood by homemakerchic.wordpress.com, Domenica by popbobshop.blogspot.com, Dooky Chase's Restaurant by creativeurbanista.wordpress.com, Drago's Seafood Restaurant by sians.blogspot.com, Elizabeth's Restaurant by hautepinkbham.com, Felix's Restauarant and Oyster Bar by Jimmy Smith, Galatoire's Restaurant by sonesta.com, Gautreau's by everybusinesslisting.com, Herbsaint Bar and Restaurant by sportsnola.com, House of Blues by stuffeyefind.com, Irene's Cuisine by adventuresinshaw.wordpress.com, The Irish House by wendyweekendgourmet.com, Jacques-Imo's Cafe by rawfocus.wordpress.com, Juan's Flying Burrito by first-bite.com, K-Paul's Louisiana Kitchen by ieee-pes-td.com, Katie's Restaurant and Bar by bruceandamy.wordpress.com, La Boca by gonola.com, Latrobe's on Royal by photoree.com, Mona's Cafe by mel-air.melissajones.org, Mulate's by gloriadellutheranic.org, The New Orleans School of Cooking by xpn.com, NOLA Restaurant by hot2molly.com, Old New Orleans Louisiana Rum Distillery by oldneworleansrum.com, Parkway Bakery and Tavern by whereyat.wordpress.com, Ralph's on the Park by ralphsonthepark.com, Robert Fresh Market by robertfreshmarket.com, Stanley by craig.purplestateofmind.com, Stella! by mirileigh.com, Surrey's Cafe and Juice Bar by joylynnkim.wordpress.com, Sylvain by hkuta.wordpress.com, Wasabi Sushi and Asian Grill by blog.timesunion.com, Ye Olde College Inn Restaurant and Bar by apleasanthouse.com

You can find us at **www.signaturetastes.com**, Facebook: **Signature Tastes of New Orleans** and on Twitter @ **Louisianasigtst**

This book is dedicated to the emergency responders...

From the first frantic call to 9-1-1
To the comforting hands at the Emergency Department
You give your time...

away from your spouses,
away from your friends,
away from children,
and yes, even from meals...

To assure all of us:

"Tonight, I will make it better for you
no matter what,
I will watch over you..."

A portion of the royalties from the sale of Signature
Tastes of New Orleans is being donated to the
following charities:

Café Reconcile
Mystic Krewe of Nyx Community Outreach
Southern Food and Beverage Museum
We humbly thank these organizations for their
contributions to the Crescent City.

I have always wondered if anyone really reads the Table of Contents. Now since this is a cookbook, I should have organized everything under its proper heading, like soups, pasta, desserts and the like. This is not just a cookbook as much as a Culinary Postcard; a celebration of the city itself...about the eateries, fine dining, casual dining, bars, and of course, the people.

Signature Tastes of NEW ORLEANS

Welcome to New Orleans: The Crescent City.................................7
The Eateries...

The Crescent City

Signature Tastes of NEW ORLEANS

When you mention New Orleans people often roll their eyes back in their head and say, "Oh, the food..." New Orleans is often associated with unique flavors, dishes and ingredients that have melded from several distinct cultures to create the delectable cuisine found in the Crescent City.

New Orleans cuisine is often associated with Creole cooking, which is known for its delicate balance of herbs, spices and sauces that enhance the flavors of the ingredients rather than overwhelming them. Creole cooking was established by 1830 and emphasizes the use of butter, cream, tomatoes, wheat flour, rich  stocks, roux and fresh herbs. The term Creole comes from the Spanish "Criollo", a name originally given to people of European descent who were born in French or Spanish colonies of the New World.

Creole cuisine was heavily influenced by the cooking habits of African slaves who were detailed to work in plantation kitchens. They were given lots of freedom to add their own touch to dishes and added spices and other unique ingredients that they were familiar within their native environment. One of their most significant contribu-

Paula Garriott, Managing Editor and Bon Vivant of New Orleans cuisine

Welcome to New Orleans

tions to the New Orleans table was the introduction of okra and its preparation in the famous gumbo now served in many restaurants and home kitchens in the Crescent City. The word gumbo is derived from the Bantu dialect's word for okra.

An equally prominent New Orleans cooking style is Cajun, often associated with country, comfort foods. Cajuns are descendents from French settlers who were forced to leave Canada in the mid-18th century when they refused to take an oath of allegiance to the British. They settled west of New Orleans in an isolated area of the swamps and bayous. Cajun cooking is thought of as hardy, home cooking and often incorporates wild meats

Creole Cooking School, 1930's

and other ingredients found in the area immediately surrounding their settlement. One-pot dishes, rich stews and etouffees often incorporate rice and dark rouxs. Pork is also commonly used in their dishes.

Immigrants to New Orleans also contributed to the stew and Italians, fleeing from poverty in Sicily, brought their Italian flavors to the new world. By the turn of the century, these new Orleanians had turned the French Quarter into the Italian Quarter--particularly in the vicinity of the French Market. They opened many businesses related to food, from grocery stores importing Italian goods to macaroni factories to restaurants. And they began celebrating St. Joseph--the patron saint of Sicily--with a joyous celebration with a lot of distinctive food.

Vietnamese immigrants, who came here in the mid-1970s, and were sponsored by the Catholic Church, have added their farming and cooking culture as well as unique flavors to the cooking pot. These include fresh Asian vegetables and fish dishes.

With the advent of refrigeration, diners in New Orleans can find crossover cuisine in most any restaurant. Crawfish, a distinctly Cajun ingredient, is now found in most any old-line Creole restaurants.

Making Groceries
New Orleans was once a Native American trading site and the high ground along the Mississippi River became a primary gathering spot for food vendors in early French New Orleans. In 1782, the first covered market in New Orleans was established along the river at Dumaine Street. In

1791 the meat market was relocated to Decatur Street between Dumaine and St. Ann, making it America's oldest public market. In 1813, as a result of damage done by hurricanes and fires, the Butchers' Market was built and still stands today, housing its oldest tenant, Café du Monde.

Through the late 19th and early 20th centuries, smaller markets sprang up across the city. By 1911, New Orleans boasted more than thirty publicly owned markets, more than any other large American city.

Private groceries, clean and refrigerated, drew customers from the old markets. New Orleans now boasts, in addition to a revived and renovated French Market, two local, Louisiana grocery chain stores, Robért Fresh Market and Rouses Supermarkets.

The popular expression, "making groceries," is derived from the French "faire son marché", "to do one's market shopping," faire translating either "to do" or "to make."

Local Ingredients
New Orleans dishes rely heavily on seasonal, locally grown ingredients, making duplication challenging for those living outside the area, but with the explosion of ingredient sourcing over the Internet, most products are

available around the country.

Vegetable farms were established upriver first by Germanic farmers recruited to Louisiana in the early 1720's. Native Americans living nearby introduced melons, beans, squash, nuts, wild game, and seafood. In the 20th century, traditional crops such as sugar, cotton, rice and
citrus were common, but new crops and cultivation included soybeans, oysters and crawfish.

Hurricane Katrina
Before the devastation wrought by Hurricane Katrina in August of 2005, there were approximately 800 restaurants in operation in New Orleans. After the storm hit the city and the levees broke, all of the restaurants were closed for a period of time during the mandatory evacuation of the city. However, many of the chefs that stayed in town opened their
freezers and put together makeshift kitchens to feed rescue workers. At the end of September, only 22 restaurants were open in the metropolitan area, which includes the north shore of Lake Pontchartrain and

Metairie. While recovery was slow, at the end of 2012, there were more than 1300 restaurants open in the city.

A surprising casualty of the storm was the family recipes passed down for generations. With eighty percent of the city under-water and most of the resi-dents' possessions destroyed, recipe books, newspaper clippings and handwritten recipes were sorely missed. Judy Walker, food editor for the Times-Picayune, and Marcelle Bienvenu, columnist, took to com-piling recipes submitted by readers and previously printed in the newspaper, to create the book, Cooking Up A Storm. The daily newspaper became the clearing-house for recipes requested by readers.

Cocktails

Legend has it that the first true cocktail, the Sazerac, was mixed in New Orleans in the early 19th century by a pharmacist named Antoine Amedee Peychaud. When Monsieur Peychaud poured the mixture of his family's recipe for stomach bitters and French brandy into double-end eggcups known as coquetiers (pronounced koh-kuh-TYAYS) the slurred pronunciation by imbibers came out like "cocktail."

Over the years, the cocktail has taken on many exotic incarnations, the most imaginative of which were concocted here in New Orleans. Famous drinks such as the Absinthe Frappe, the Ramos Gin Fizz, and the Obituary Cocktail, the Hurricane, the Hand Grenade and many others owe their beginnings to the imagination and creativity of New Orleans bartenders. We have included some of our favorite cocktails in this edition.

Unique ingredients

New Orleans cuisine relies on unique ingredients some of which may not be available in reader locales. We have compiled a list of close substitutes for your convenience, but for best results with the recipes included in this cookbook, we recommend ordering the ingredients online from their source. Or better yet, travel to New Orleans and bring the ingredients home.

Abita Beer – a New Orleans beer that is distributed around the country. Look for it at Whole Foods or Total Wine and More. The company has a list of national distributors on their website, www.abita.com. Substitute a regular medium light beer.

Andouille Sausage – a coarse-grained, heavily spiced, smoked pork sausage. Found in Whole Foods markets or under the Johnsonville brand in most locations. Also known as Louisiana-style or Creole-style.

Boudin Sausage - A white sausage made of pork without the blood. A poor substitute would be weisswurst or bratwurst.

Creole or Cajun Seasoning – Every New Orleanian has their favorite brand of this seasoning, which generally contains cayenne pepper, black pepper, paprika, garlic and onion powder, thyme and oregano. They can be purchased with or without salt. These can be found in your local supermarket in the spice section. Popular brands include Tony Chachere's, Zatarain's and Emeril's.

Café du Monde beignet mix – Is now available in many markets in the ethnic food section. It is also available at

Cost Plus World Market or online.

Cane Vinegar – Cane vinegar is mild vinegar made from sugar cane. Unseasoned Japanese rice wine vinegar is an adequate substitute.

Crawfish – Also known as crayfish and crawdads, these miniature lobster-looking crustaceans are available fresh seasonally around the country. While we don't recommend frozen crawfish, if you must use them, make sure you get the best quality available. Check with your local seafood market.

Creole Mustard – coarse-ground mustard known for its high concentration of mustard seeds. Whole-grain mustard can be substituted, but several brands of Creole mustard are available nationally.

Creole Tomato – Creole Tomatoes are vine-ripened tomatoes developed by Louisiana State University around 1956. It was developed to thrive in hot, humid climates. It yields a 3", round, firm, red fruit with lots of juice and a delicious tomato flavor with good acidity. If you have to substitute these, choose the largest, ugliest heirloom tomatoes you can find in your local supermarket or Farmer's Market.

Filé Powder – also known as Gumbo Filé, this is a spicy powder made of dried, ground sassafras leaves. Filé is available in the spice or ethnic section of most markets.

French Bread – New Orleans French bread is crispy on the outside and light and fluffy on the inside. For a similar taste, by fresh baked French bread available daily in most supermarkets or local French bakeries.

Grits – While this used to be available only in Southern states, we are confident you will be able to find both quick and regular grits in your local market.

Holy Trinity – Similar to the French mire poix, which consists of onion, carrot and celery, the New Orleans Holy Trinity, referred to in many Cajun dishes, is comprised of bell pepper, onion and celery.

Louisiana Rice – Louisiana rice is long-grain rice that cooks up fluffy and separate. Good quality long-grain white rice can be substituted.

Mirliton – a pear-shaped vegetable. Substitute chayote.

Plantain – firmer and less sweet than a banana, plantains are found in specialty produce sections. Bananas can be substituted with less than optimal results; cooking time should be adjusted to retain firmness.

Red Beans and Black Eyed Peas – Camellia Brand beans seem to be a favorite for their uniform shape, but good quality kidney bean can be substituted.

Remoulade or rémoulade - invented in France, is a popular condiment in many countries. Very much like the tartar sauce of some English-speaking cultures, remoulade is often aioli- or mayonnaise-based. Although similar to tartar sauce, it is often more yellowish (or reddish in Louisiana), often flavored with curry, and sometimes contains chopped pickles or piccalilli. It can also contain horseradish, paprika, anchovies, capers and a host of other items.

Roux – A roux is commonly used in New Orleans cooking and consists of a thickening agent, often flour or filé, cooked with a fat, such as lard, butter or cooking oil. Many New Orleans recipes begin with "First you make a roux." Cooking the roux longer to make it darker creates the color of the roux, often mentioned in recipe directions. Roux is often referred to as light or blonde, medium or dark.

Seafood – The best seafood is found in the Gulf of Mexico, south of the city, however, not every location is lucky enough to have access to these succulent morsels. According to the Louisiana Seafood site more than 1/3 of the nation's seafood comes from Louisiana waters. We recommend that you get the freshest seafood available for the best results.

Steen's Cane Syrup – syrup made from sugar cane. Karo dark corn syrup can be used as a substitute.

Sweetbreads – While not a uniquely New Orleans cut of meat, many people are unfamiliar with them. They are cut from the thymus and pancreas of a calf or lamb and can be special ordered from most meat departments.

Tabasco Sauce – Many of the recipes in this cookbook mention Tabasco brand hot sauce in their ingredients. Even New Orleanians have a preference in their hot sauce, so feel free to use your favorite brand. Also known as Louisiana-style hot sauce.

RECIPES
&
RESTAURANTS

BBQ Shrimp BLT

Named for its 555 Canal Street location in the New Orleans Marriott, this trendy restaurant serves a mouthwatering menu incorporating New Orleans, Cajun, French, American and Creole cuisine. Unique menu items include surf and turf sliders, Creole brown butter mashed potatoes and this New Orleans Wine and Food Experience award-winning dish.

Sandwich:
1 lb. (21/25 count) Louisiana shrimp, peeled & deveined
6 slices thick-cut bacon
Creole tomato
head bibb lettuce
2 brioche twist rolls
Creole Barbecue Sauce

Creole Barbecue Sauce:
1½ tsp black pepper
1 tsp salt
1 tsp onion powder
1 tsp garlic powder
½ tsp white pepper
½ tsp cayenne pepper
½ lb. bacon, minced
1½ C. onion, chopped
2 C. chicken stock
1½ C. ketchup
2 C. Creole tomatoes, chopped
1 C. pinot noir
1 C. honey
5 Tbsp orange juice, fresh squeezed
2 Tbsp lemon juice, fresh squeezed
2 tsp minced garlic
1 tsp Tabasco
stick unsalted butter

Sandwich:
1. Grill shrimp and then finish in a sauté pan with the Creole Barbeque Sauce.

2. Pile high on the twist bun with thick cut bacon and finish with sliced Creole tomato and bibb lettuce.

Creole Barbecue Sauce:
1. Fry bacon until crisp. Stir in onion. Cover until tender.

2. Stir in seasonings. Cook until expanded.

3. Add stock, ketchup, Creole tomatoes, pinot noir, honey, orange and lemon juices, garlic and Tabasco. Simmer for twenty minutes.

4. Remove from heat and stir in butter.

"Creole is New Orleans city food."
Paul Prudhomme

Blackened Stuffed Pork Tenderloin, Dirty Rice and Chayote Slaw

Signature Tastes of NEW ORLEANS

Imaginative but approachable food is served in this contemporary restaurant in the Wyndham Riverfront New Orleans Hotel. Enjoy a cocktail at sidewalk tables or settle into cushy banquettes for your night on the town. Classic New Orleans dishes, like fried oyster po'boy and cochon de lait grace the menu, as well as nouvelle cuisine.

Pork and Stuffing:
pork tenderloin
¼ C. celery
¼ C. red bell pepper
¼ C. shallots
¼ C. onion
2 chipotle peppers
1 tsp chili powder
1 tsp cumin
1½ qt. chicken stock
1½ qt. breadcrumbs

Chayote Slaw:
1 mirliton
1 red bell pepper
½ C. red cabbage
½ jalapeno
¼ C. sugar
¼ C. cider vinegar
2 Tbsp salt
1 C. mayonnaise

Dirty Rice:
1 red bell pepper
1 green bell pepper
5 onions
5 stalks celery
¼ link andouille sausage
5 C. pecans
1 bulb garlic
1 Tbsp thyme
1 Tbsp marjoram
1 Tbsp fennel seed
1 Tbsp celery seed
1 Tbsp coriander
1 Tbsp cayenne pepper
salt to taste
pepper to taste
5 qt. rice
½ lb. chicken livers
1 qt. chicken stock

Pork and Stuffing:
1. Sauté celery, red bell pepper, shallots, onion and chipotles until soft.
2. Add seasonings and deglaze with chicken stock.
3. Let the mixture come to a boil and add breadcrumbs. Stir.
4. Remove from heat and cover.
5. Clean pork tenderloin and filet open. Pound flat.
6. After stuffing has cooled, place in middle of tenderloin. Roll up and tie.
7. Bake in 350°F oven until internal temperature of tenderloin reads 165°F on a meat thermometer.

Chayote Slaw:
1. Julienne mirliton, red bell pepper, jalapeno and cabbage.
2. Mix sugar, vinegar and salt with mayonnaise.
3. Combine vegetables and dressing.

Dirty Rice:
1. Sauté first seven ingredients until tender.
2. Add seasonings and mix thoroughly.
3. Poach chicken livers in stock for five minutes. Remove and reserve liquid.
4. Mince livers and add to vegetables.
5. Add chicken stock to rice and cook on stove.
6. Once rice is cooked, fold in livers and vegetables.
7. Adjust seasoning if needed.

701 Convention Center Drive, (Wyndham Riverfront New Orleans)

7 on Fulton

"In America, I would say New York and New Orleans are the two most interesting food towns. In New Orleans, they don't have a bad deli. There's no mediocrity accepted."
Mario Batali

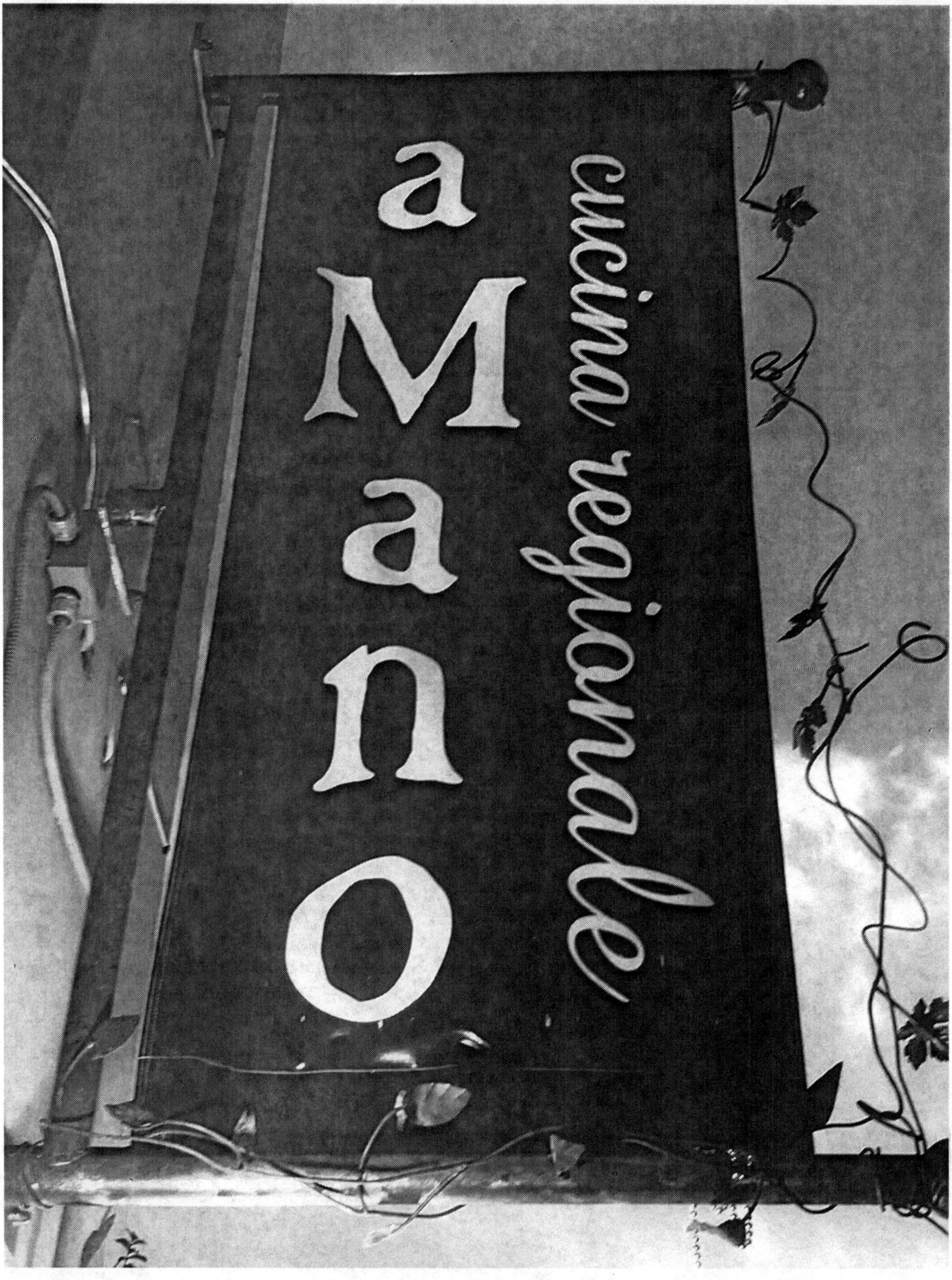
aMano
cucina regionale

Orecchiette Pugliese

Critically acclaimed Chef Adolfo Garcia's newest restaurant, a Mano, serves central and southern Italian cuisine. House-cured salami, handcrafted pastas and long-simmered dishes highlight the menu in this warm and welcoming trattoria. Using local, sustainable and artisanal ingredients, Garcia and chef-partner Joshua Smith create memorable, multi-course Italian meals sure to please the most sophisticated palate.

1 lb. orecchiette pasta
4 cloves garlic, finely chopped
½ lb. Italian sausage, casings removed and crumbled
¼ C. sundried tomatoes, julienned
1 lb. broccoli florets or chopped broccoli rabé
¼ C. plus 2 Tbsp extra-virgin olive oil
½ C. white wine
¼ tsp hot red pepper flakes
salt to taste
1 C. ricotta salata cheese, grated

1. Cook broccoli in boiling salted water until tender but still firm to bite.

2. Cook orecchiette in large pot of boiling salted water until pasta is tender but still firm to bite. Drain pasta, reserving one-half cup of the pasta water.

3. In a heavy-bottomed pan, heat two tablespoons olive oil. Add the crumbled Italian sausage and garlic and cook through.

4. Add the red pepper flakes, sundried tomatoes and white wine to the pan and continue cooking until most of the wine has evaporated.

5. Add the broccoli, orrechiette, and the reserved pasta water to the pan and toss it all together.

6. Remove pan from heat and stir in one-fourth cup extra-virgin olive oil and salt to taste.

7. Transfer to a large bowl and served topped with grated ricotta salata.

a Mano
870 Tchoupitoulas Street

"Like Venice, Italy, New Orleans is a cultural treasure."
Ed McMahon

Abita Beer Bread

Signature Tastes of NEW ORLEANS

Founded in 1986 Abita Brewing Company is located thirty miles north of New Orleans. Brewing over 125,000 barrels of beer and 8,000 barrels of root beer, Abita products are available around the country. Stop by the brewery and take a tour of their state-of-the-art facility and taste some of their seasonal brews. The pub, located in downtown Abita Springs, was the original home of Abita Brewery and offers some of the finest pub food available.

1 C. Abita beer, any type or seasonal, at room temperature
½ Tbsp oil
2 Tbsp granulated sugar
¾ tsp salt
2¾ C. all-purpose flour
1 pkg. active dry yeast, (2¼ tsp)

1. Add the ingredients to a bread machine in order.

2. Set on basic bread setting on machine.

3. Follow manufacturer's instructions for making bread in particular machine.

Abita Brew Pub
72011 Holly Street, Abita Springs

"New Orleans has a personality unlike any other city,... It is relaxed, and a high percentage of the population knows the value of a good meal, a good laugh, some cold beer and crawfish, and a good band."
Tom Piazza

Oysters Louisiana

Acme Oyster House opened its doors in 1910 and has been serving some of the city's best oysters ever since. They offer a variety of preparations for their oysters, including ice cold on the half shell, char-grilled, fried, in po' boys and in soup. They also offer other New Orleans traditional dishes such as gumbo, jambalaya and bread pudding. Diners who can eat fifteen dozen oysters or more in one hour are awarded a t-shirt, hat and a place on the wall of fame.

4 oz. butter, melted	**1.** Melt butter in a skillet.
1½ pt. oysters, drained	**2.** Add oysters and cook until dry.
4 green onions, chopped finely	**3.** Add onions and garlic and cook slowly for at least ten minutes.
3 cloves garlic, minced	**4.** Fold in crabmeat and crumbs.
½ lb. fresh lump crabmeat	**5.** Simmer five minutes more.
½ C. bread crumbs	**6.** Add salt and pepper to taste.
salt to taste	
pepper to taste	

"He was a bold man that first ate an oyster."
Jonathan Swift

Sweet Potato Praline Casserole

Alex Patout's Louisiana Restaurant, located in the historic French Quarter, gives diners a choice of two dining rooms or a table on the terrace, where they can dine on the best in Cajun cuisine. Patout was born and raised in New Iberia, Louisiana, the heart of Cajun country. He was named one of the top chefs by Food and Wine Magazine in 1985 and has won numerous other accolades. After Hurricane Katrina, Alex Patout's was one of the French Quarter restaurants that opened make-shift kitchens to feed rescue and relief workers.

Signature Tastes of NEW ORLEANS

Alex Patout's Louisiana Restaurant
720 Saint Louis Street

5 large sweet potatoes or yams
⅓ C. milk
½ C. (¼ lb.) softened butter
½ C. heavy cream
½ C. sugar
1 C. light brown sugar
2 eggs, beaten
⅓ C. melted butter
1 tsp vanilla
1 C. chopped pecans

1. Preheat oven to 350°F.
2. Scrub the sweet potatoes (or yams) well and place them in the oven.
3. Bake until tender, about forty minutes, and remove.
4. When cool enough to handle, halve and scoop out the insides into a large mixing bowl. Mash well. (Should yield about three cups.)
5. Mix the softened butter into the mashed sweet potatoes (or yams) along with the sugar, eggs, vanilla, and milk.
6. Pour the mixture into a baking pan or casserole dish.
7. Bring the cream to a simmer in a small saucepan.
8. Add the brown sugar and stir until it dissolves.
9. Cook the mixture over medium heat until it reaches the soft-ball stage on a candy thermometer.
10. Remove from heat and beat in the butter and the chopped pecans.
11. Pour the brown sugar mixture over the sweet potatoes (or yams) in the baking pan.
12. Bake until very hot and beginning to brown.

"My dream is to become a farmer. Just a bohemian guy pulling up his own sweet potatoes for dinner."
Lenny Kravitz

Braised Pork Tacos

The American Sector, one of chef John Besh's classic restaurants, serves American comfort food with a sassy spin. Known for its generous portions, vintage cocktails and unique location, The American Sector serves lunch and dinner at the National World War II Museum. Founded by historian and author, Stephen Ambrose, the museum tells the story of the American experience in World War II. Veterans of the war that changed the world are given the royal treatment when visiting the museum and the restaurant.

Signature Tastes of NEW ORLEANS

945 Magazine Street, (National World War II Museum)

The American Sector

Pork:
3 lb. boneless pork butt
kosher salt
2 Tbsp cayenne pepper
2 Tbsp chili powder
2 Tbsp smoked paprika
1 Tbsp ground cumin
1 Tbsp garlic powder
1 Tbsp onion powder
2 large yellow onions, roughly chopped
2 jalapenos, thinly sliced crosswise
zest of 3 limes

Guacamole:
3 Hass avocados—halved, pitted and chopped
juice of 2 limes
1 medium red onion, finely chopped
1 jalapeno, finely chopped
1 C. finely chopped fresh cilantro
1 tsp reserved taco spice blend
kosher salt, to taste

Tomatoes:
3 ripe medium tomatoes, finely chopped
1 C. finely chopped fresh cilantro
juice of 2 limes
kosher salt

Tacos:
12 fresh corn tortillas (preferably white corn tortillas)
6 scallions, trimmed and halved lengthwise
kosher salt
grapeseed oil
½ lime
6 radishes, trimmed (preferably breakfast radishes)
1 C. crumbled queso fresco cheese

Pork:
1. Preheat the oven to 300°F.
2. Place the pork butt on a cutting board and generously season all over with kosher salt.
3. In a medium bowl, whisk together the cayenne, chili powder, smoked paprika, cumin, garlic powder and onion powder. Measure one teaspoon of the mixture and set aside (for the guacamole); rub the rest of the spice blend into all sides of the meat.
4. In a heavy-bottomed pot set over medium-high heat, bring the pork, onions, jalapenos, lime zest and eight cups water to a boil. Turn off the heat, cover and transfer the pot to the oven. Cook until a fork easily slides into the center of the pork and you can twist the fork with little to no resistance, about three hours. Remove from the oven, uncover and set aside until cool enough to shred. Taste and season with salt if needed.

Guacamole:
1. In a large bowl, use a fork to lightly mash the avocados with the lime juice.
2. Add the onion, jalapeno, cilantro, reserved taco spice blend and salt and stir until the mixture is semi-smooth. Taste and adjust the salt if needed. Cover with plastic wrap and refrigerate.

Tomatoes:
1. In a medium bowl, stir together the tomatoes, cilantro, lime juice and salt to taste. Set aside.

Assembly:
1. Stack the tortillas and wrap in a sheet of aluminum foil.
2. Place the tortillas on top of the oven to warm (or reduce the oven temperature to 200°F and place the tortillas in the oven just until warmed, three to five minutes).
3. In a medium bowl, toss the scallions with some salt and a drizzle of oil.
4. Heat a heavy-bottomed skillet or a cast-iron skillet over high heat for two minutes.
5. Add the scallions and brown on all sides, four to five minutes total.
6. Turn off the heat and season with a squeeze of lime juice and salt to taste.
7. Fill a medium bowl with ice and water.
8. Use a vegetable peeler to shave the radishes.
9. Place the shavings in the bowl to stay crisp.
10. Set the warm tortillas on a platter.
11. To serve, fill a warm tortilla with some shredded pork. Top with guacamole, seasoned tomatoes, seared scallions, shaved radish and queso fresco.

"An army marches on its stomach."
Napolean

Cantaloupe Italian Ice

This New Orleans landmark has been serving Italian ice cream and desserts since 1905, when young Angelo Brocato opened the Ice Cream Parlor and put to use the techniques he learned as a boy in Palermo, Italy. Made daily on the premises, Brocato's ice creams use only the freshest and purest ingredients and recipes handed down for generations. Twenty-four flavors of ice cream, Italian ices, spumoni, cassata, coffee and cannoli are featured daily.

1 qt. (32 ounces) water
1¼ lb. sugar
1 lemon, juiced
2 medium-sized ripe cantaloupes

1. Dissolve sugar and water in a two-quart saucepan over medium-high heat. Bring to a boil and cook for two minutes. Remove from the heat and cool.
2. Peel and seed the cantaloupes. Cut into two-inch pieces.
3. Puree in a food processor.
4. Strain through a medium sieve.
5. Mix strained cantaloupe juice, sugar syrup and lemon juice with a wire whisk.
6. Pour into an ice cream machine.
7. Add some cantaloupe pulp, if desired.
8. Freeze to a smooth consistency, according to manufacturer's directions.
9. Place in the freezer compartment of refrigerator for a few hours to harden.
10. Serve in a dessert glass topped with whipped cream or with a scoop of vanilla ice cream.
11. Garnish with fresh mint leaves.

Signature Tastes of NEW ORLEANS

Angelo Brocato's
214 North Carrollton Avenue

"Angelo Brocato's is the sweet side of New Orleans' red-gravy roots."
Judy Walker

Shrimp Creole

For more than 160 years, Antoine's Restaurant's excellent French-Creole cuisine, superb service and unique atmosphere have delighted both locals and tourists. Home of the original Oysters Rockefeller, so named for it's rich sauce, Antoine's has fourteen uniquely styled dining rooms that house memorabilia from many notable guests including General Patton, President Roosevelt and Pope John Paul the II.

2 lb. shrimp, peeled
5 Tbsp butter, divided
1 C. green bell pepper, chopped
1 C. onion, chopped
2 (14 oz.) cans tomatoes with juice
¼ tsp thyme
4 cloves garlic
2 tsp parsley, chopped
1 tsp paprika
2 bay leaves
salt to taste
cayenne pepper to taste
1 Tbsp cornstarch
cooked white rice for serving

1. Sauté green pepper and onion in two tablespoons butter

2. Add tomatoes and juice and other seasonings.

3. Blend in the cornstarch using a wire whisk.

4. Simmer covered one hour.

5. Sauté the shrimp in three tablespoons butter that has been seasoned with salt and pepper.

6. Add shrimp to the sauce.

7. Remove bay leaves and serve with cooked white rice.

NOTE: This is better if made a day ahead and can also be frozen.

Antoine's Restaurant
713 Saint Louis Street

"Shrimp is the fruit of the sea. You can barbecue it, boil it, broil it, bake it, sauté it. There's, um, shrimp kebabs, shrimp Creole, shrimp gumbo, pan fried, deep fried, stir fried. There's pineapple shrimp and lemon shrimp, coconut shrimp, pepper shrimp, shrimp soup, shrimp stew, shrimp salad, shrimp and potatoes, shrimp burger, shrimp sandwich... That's, that's about it."
Bubba Blue

Turtle Soup

Since its inception in 1918, Arnaud's has remained true to its traditions and courtesies. Offering live Dixieland Jazz in the Jazz Bistro, romantic dinners in the Main Dining Room, cocktails in the award winning French 75 Bar and an assortment of private French Quarter fine dining rooms, Arnaud's offers the quintessential New Orleans dining experience.

1 gal. water
3 lb. turtle meat or veal shoulder, or a combination of both, including any bones available
3 bay leaves
3 whole cloves
zest of 1 lemon
1 Tbsp kosher or sea salt
½ tsp whole black peppercorns
1 C. unsalted butter
⅔ C. all-purpose flour
2 stalks celery, chopped
2 medium onions, chopped
1 small green bell pepper, stemmed, seeded, de-ribbed and chopped
2 cloves garlic, finely chopped
½ tsp fresh thyme leaves or ¼ tsp dried thyme
½ teaspoon chopped fresh marjoram or ¼ teaspoon dried marjoram
1 C. dry sherry
2 Tbsp Worcestershire sauce
1 C. tomato puree
1 tsp. salt-free Creole seasoning
½ tsp. Tabasco Sauce
2 hard-cooked eggs, chopped
leaves only from 1 bunch of flat-leaf parsley, well washed and chopped
5 oz. fresh baby spinach (about 4 C, loosely packed) well washed and chopped

1. In a large stock pot, cover the turtle meat with the water and add the bay leaves, cloves, lemon zest, salt and black peppercorns.
2. Place over high heat and bring to a boil, then immediately reduce the heat so water simmers gently. Cook slowly for two hours.
3. Strain the stock, reserving the liquid and the meat separately. If necessary, add stock to make three quarts.
4. When cool enough to handle, chop and shred the meat into small pieces and set aside.
5. In a large saucepan, use the butter and flour to make a medium-dark roux the color of a well-used penny.
6. When roux reaches the correct color, add the celery, onions, bell pepper and garlic, and cook, stirring occasionally, until the vegetables are soft, about seven minutes.
7. Add the thyme, marjoram, sherry, Worcestershire sauce and tomato puree and bring the mixture to a boil.
8. Lower the heat and add the Creole seasoning and Tabasco. Whisk in the reserved stock and add the turtle meat. Simmer the mixture, stirring occasionally, for thirty minutes.
9. Taste for seasoning and adjust with salt, freshly ground black pepper and/or Tabasco Sauce as desired.
10. Add parsley and spinach leaves and simmer for ten minutes more.
11. Serve in wide, shallow bowls.
12. A splash of sherry poured at the table brings out the richness of the turtle soup. The addition of sherry is another local point of difference. Some cooks add the sherry during the cooking process, others when it is served and some prefer their turtle soup with no sherry at all.

Arnaud's
813 Bienville Avenue

"Blues is the soupbone in the soup."
Nanette Workman

Vintner's Chicken

Atchafalaya Restaurant is the perfect choice for those wanting a memorable meal in the historic Irish Channel neighborhood. Serving contemporary Creole cuisine, Atchafalaya prides itself on attentive service and warm hospitality. Open for lunch and dinner, the weekend brunches feature a "Bloody Mary Bar" with a variety of hot sauces and vegetables to jazz up your eye-opener.

2 Tbsp plain flour ¼ tsp basil, crumbled ¼ tsp dried tarragon, crumbled ¼ tsp paprika 4 chicken breast halves, boned and skinned 1 Tbsp safflower oil 1 Tbsp butter 2 small cloves of garlic, minced ½ C. white wine (dry) 1 C. red seedless grapes, halved ½ C. chicken broth 1 tsp fresh lemon juice salt and freshly ground pepper, to taste 1 Tbsp chopped freshly picked parsley for garnish	**1.** Mix flour, basil, tarragon, paprika, salt and pepper in large bowl. **2.** Add chicken and toss gently to coat. **3.** Heat oil and butter in large heavy skillet over medium high heat. **4.** Stir in garlic. Cook only a few seconds before adding chicken. Sauté on both sides until golden brown. **5.** Pour in wine. Cover and cook until chicken is done, about five minutes. **6.** Add grapes, broth and lemon juice and heat through. **7.** Transfer chicken and grapes to a platter using slotted spoon. **8.** Reduce sauce by about half. **9.** Pour over chicken, garnish with parsley and serve.

Atchafalaya Restaurant
901 Louisiana Avenue

"The first time I was cooking for my wife, Stephanie, way before she was my wife, I actually put three chickens on the rotisserie and I closed the grill, which is really a bad idea. But I just wasn't thinking very straight that day. And I looked outside and I saw, like, smoke and flames."
Bobby Flay

The "Perfect" Afternoon

2 oz. Perfect vodka
1½ oz. fresh honeydew melon juice
½ oz. simple syrup
½ oz. St. Germain
¼ oz. fresh lime juice
6 large mint leaves
1 oz. soda water

1. Muddle simple syrup and mint.

2. Add all additional ingredients, except for soda water and shake.

3. Top with soda water.

Signature Tastes of NEW ORLEANS

Bar Tonique
820 North Rampart Street

"Once we hit forty, women only have about four taste buds left: one for vodka, one for wine, one for cheese, and one for chocolate."
Gina Barreca

Garlic Soup

Susan Spicer's French Quarter gem delights diners with five-star service in one of its tastefully decorated dining rooms or on their lovely garden patio. The cuisine varies seasonally, with hints of Mediterranean, the Far East, North Africa, France, Italy and the United States. Her signature dishes include goat cheese crouton with mushrooms in Madeira cream, Covey Rise Farm duck breast and confit crepe with date molasses and pistachios, as well as this wonderful soup.

2 Tbsp olive oil 2 Tbsp butter 2 lb. onion (about 4), chopped 2 C. garlic cloves (about 4 large heads), chopped 2 qt. chicken stock or canned low-sodium chicken broth ½ loaf day-old French bread (about ¼ lb.) cut into chunks 1 bouquet garni (6 parsley stems, 9 sprigs fresh or 1½ tsp dried thyme and 1 bay leaf) 1½ tsp salt 2 C. half-and-half ¼ tsp fresh-ground black pepper croutons, optional	**1.** In a large pot, heat the oil and butter over low heat. **2.** Add the onions and garlic. Cover and cook, stirring occasionally, until very soft and beginning to turn golden, about thirty minutes. **3.** Raise the heat to moderate and continue cooking the onions and garlic, uncovered, stirring frequently, until deep golden, about ten minutes longer. **4.** Add the stock, bread, bouquet garni, and salt. Bring to a boil. **5.** Reduce the heat and simmer about fifteen minutes. **6.** Remove the bouquet garni and puree the soup in a blender or food processor. **7.** Strain the soup back into the pot. **8.** Add the half-and-half and pepper and bring back to a boil. **9.** Serve topped with the croutons, if you like.

Bayona
430 Dauphine Street

"Garlic used as it should be used is the soul, the divine essence, of cookery. The cook who can employ it successfully will be found to possess the delicacy of perception, the accuracy of judgment, and the dexterity of hand which go to the formation of a great artist."
Mrs. W. G. Waters

Akara-Black-Eyed Pea Fritters with Coconut Oil and Pepper Sauce

New Orleans has always been considered one of the most amazing culinary melting pots in the United States and Bennachin Restaurant brings that home with cuisine from Cameroon and Gambia. On Royal Street, Bennachin is located in a quiet area, off the beaten path. Offering vegetarian dishes as well as those that will delight a carnivore palate, this unique restaurant is worth a stop on any culinary journey of The Big Easy.

1 C. dried black-eyed peas, sorted, soaked overnight, drained, and rinsed
½ medium onion, diced
½ C. raw peanuts
1 tsp minced thyme
¼ tsp cayenne pepper
1 Tbsp apple cider vinegar
¼ C. plus 2 Tbsp water
1 tsp coarse sea salt
½ C. finely chopped green bell pepper
1 Tbsp cornmeal
5 C. coconut oil

1. Remove the skins from the beans by adding them to a large bowl, filling the bowl with water, agitating the beans, and fishing out the skins that float to the top with a fine mesh strainer. Rinse beans well.

2. In a food processor fitted with a metal blade, combine the beans, onion, peanuts, thyme, cayenne, vinegar, water and salt, and pulse until completely smooth. Transfer to a medium bowl, cover, and refrigerate for one hour.

3. Preheat the oven to 200°F.

4. Remove the batter from the refrigerator, add the bell pepper and cornmeal, and beat with a wooden spoon for two minutes.

5. In a medium-size saucepan over high heat, warm the coconut oil until hot but not smoking, about five minutes.

Bennachin Restaurant
1212 Royal Street

"Does eating black-eyed peas on New Year's Day bring good fortune in the coming year? WHO CARES? They're just good eatin'! But since I only make them once or twice a year, I may as well make them on January the 1st."
Johnny L.A.

American Kobe Flat Iron Steak

Besh Steakhouse at Harrah's Casino
8 Canal Street, (Harrah's New Orleans)

Native son John Besh has a franchise of restaurants throughout the city, but this one in Harrah's casino specializes in steaks that melt in your mouth. In a contemporary setting high rollers (or those who aspire to be) can dine in comfort away from the clang of the casino floor. Besh sets himself apart from other restaurateurs in the area in that he encourages his staff to give back to the community and practices what he preaches with the Chefs Move! Initiative of the John Besh Foundation. He offers recipients of the award a full scholarship to The French Culinary Institute of Manhattan and internship in a New York kitchen with the hope of honing young chefs and broadening their horizons.

Peppers:
small piquillo peppers
3 C. lobster meat, small dice (roughly 2 one-pound lobsters)
3 C. shrimp, small dice
¾ lb. cream cheese
3 Tbsp chives
½ lb. mascarpone cheese
½ lb. goat cheese
2 Tbsp fresh lemon juice
½ C. dry breadcrumbs
salt to taste
freshly ground pepper to taste

Sauce:
½ lb. cleaned oxtails
large carrot, large dice
2 stalks celery, large dice
large onion, large dice
1 Tbsp tomato paste
1 C. red wine
bay leaf
sprig fresh thyme
1 qt. veal demi-glace
¼ C. olive oil

Whipped Potatoes:
5 large Yukon Gold potatoes, peeled and roughly chopped
½ lb. butter
½ qt. heavy whipping cream
½ C. goat cheese
salt to taste
freshly ground pepper to taste

Garnish and Plating:
Kobe beef flatiron steak
3 C. fried sage
½ C. fresh herb oil

Peppers:
1. Lightly sauté the seafood in a pan and fold into the cream cheese.
2. Season the mixture with chives, salt and pepper and stuff into the peppers.
3. Reserve.

Whipped Potatoes:
1. In a large pot of water, bring the potatoes to a simmer and cook until soft, then strain.
2. In another small pot, combine the butter, heavy cream and goat cheese and cook until cheese is incorporated.
3. Mash the potatoes and fold in the cheese mixture.
4. Season with salt and pepper.

Sauce:
1. Season the oxtails with salt and pepper and sear in a heavy bottomed pot with the oil.
2. When the oxtails have a nice brown color, remove the oxtails and add the vegetables. Caramelize for five minutes.
3. Add the tomato paste and red wine. Let the wine reduce by half.
4. Place the oxtails back into the pot and add the veal stock.
5. Cover the pan and let roast in an oven for three hours at 350°F.
6. Drain off the liquid and season with salt and pepper.

Plating:
1. Season the Kobe steaks with salt and pepper, then grill.
2. Place the Whipped Potatoes in the center of the plate and top with the sliced Kobe.
3. Drizzle the Sauce around the plate and place the Stuffed Peppers on top of the meat.
4. Drizzle the plate with herb oil and garnish with fried sage.

"When I speak of one of our chefs doing good acts through food it's not about Besh, but it's about what we can all do each day."
Chef John Besh

Grilled Sweetbreads and Zucchini with Roasted Pepper and Brown Butter Coulis

Bistro Daisy is a small Uptown restaurant named after restaurateurs Anton and Diane Schulte's daughter. Serving fresh, seasonal and (when available) local foods in the American bistro style. Located in a classic shotgun house on Magazine Street, Bistro Daisy serves dishes such as crawfish ravioli, duck breast, a daily fish special and is a spot that locals and tourists agree is a don't miss.

Sweetbreads:
2 qt. water
juice of 1 lemon
2 bay leaves
kosher salt, to taste
1 lb. sweetbreads,
soaked in milk overnight

Red Onion:
½ small red onion,
julienne
salt, to taste

Roasted Pepper and Brown Butter Coulis:
red pepper, roasted,
peeled, and seeded
1 Tbsp apple cider
vinegar
1 Tbsp honey
2 tsp Dijon mustard
½ C. butter, browned
slowly in a sauté pan
salt, to taste
freshly ground black
pepper, to taste

To Assemble and Serve:
oil
salt, to taste
freshly ground black
pepper, to taste
1 large zucchini, peeled,
seeded, and julienne
¾ C. chopped rendered
apple-smoked bacon
¼ bunch fresh Italian
parsley, chiffonade

Sweetbreads:
1. Combine the water, lemon juice, and bay leaves in a large pot and simmer; season with the salt.
2. Drain the sweetbreads and poach in the broth.
3. Remove from the liquid and shock in an ice bath until completely cooled.
4. Remove as much membrane from the sweetbreads as possible while keeping them in pieces large enough to grill.

Red Onion:
1. Generously salt the red onion.
2. Allow to stand for thirty minutes, then rinse under cold water for thirty seconds. Set aside.

Roasted Pepper and Brown Butter Coulis:
1. Put the roasted red pepper, vinegar, honey, and Dijon mustard in a blender and puree.
2. With the blender running, slowly pour in the brown butter to form an emulsion.
3. Season with salt and pepper.

To Assemble and Serve:
1. Oil and season the sweetbreads; grill over medium-high heat until browned.
2. Oil, season, and grill the zucchini.
3. Toss in a mixing bowl with the red onion, bacon, zucchini, and half the coulis.
4. Divide into four portions on appetizer plates.
5. Garnish with the parsley and the remaining sauce.

Bistro Daisy
5831 Magazine Street

"I feel a recipe is only a theme, which an intelligent cook can play each time with variation."
Madame Benoit

Chicken Saltimbocca

Signature Tastes of NEW ORLEANS

This restaurant is reminiscent of a classic British gentleman's club and is famous for its Nouveau Creole cuisine. Tucked away in a quite corner of the French Quarter in the Prince Conti Hotel, it is hard to imagine you are only a half block away from Bourbon Street. Live music on the weekends and one of the best martinis in town make this a fine place to start your French Quarter evening.

four 8 oz. free-range chicken breasts, split, trimmed and slightly pounded *½ C. flour, seasoned with kosher salt and fresh ground black pepper* *¼ C. oil blend, (80% salad oil and 20% olive oil)* *1½ C. shiitake mushrooms, sliced* *3 Tbsp shallots, fine diced* *2 Tbsp garlic, minced* *2 Tbsp fresh sage, fine diced* *1 Tbsp kosher salt* *1 Tbsp fresh ground black pepper* *4 oz. imported prosciutto, thinly sliced and julienne* *8 oz. Marsala wine* *4 oz. veal glaze* *2 oz. unsalted butter, softened*

1. Dust chicken with the seasoned flour, removing excess flour, set aside.

2. Heat oil in a large sauté pan; add chicken breasts, sauté two minutes over high heat.

3. Flip chicken breasts and add shallots, garlic, sage, salt, pepper and prosciutto. Sauté for another minute or two.

4. Deglaze the pan with Marsala wine, let cook for one minute and add veal glaze. Turn down heat to medium and simmer for two to four minutes, turning chicken once. Note: For more sauce, add a few more ounces of veal glaze.

5. Remove the chicken from the pan and reduce sauce for another two to three minutes, whisk in butter and pour over chicken breasts.

6. Serving suggestions: Serve with garlic or chive mashed potatoes and garnish with fresh chives.

The Bombay Club
830 Conti Street, (Prince Conti Hotel)

"And believe me, a good piece of chicken can make anybody believe in the existence of God."
Sherman Alexie

Crabmeat Imperial

Housed in the historical 1840's Natchez building, within earshot of boat whistles on the Mississippi, Bon Ton Cafe serves Cajun food prepared stylishly from original family recipes. Two specialties of the house prepared as only the Bon Ton knows how - its famed Rum Ramsey cocktail adapted from a recipe handed down from the early 1900's and known only to the owners, and its Bread Pudding with Whiskey Sauce that is so delicious it verges on being wicked.

2 lb. fresh picked jumbo lump crabmeat
1 C. green onions, chopped with bulbs and stems
¼ C. pimentos, chopped
1 C. olive oil
½ C. sliced mushrooms
½ C. sherry wine
¼ C. chopped parsley
salt to taste
12 toasted bread points – from French bread cut in lengths to a point (toast points should be approximately 4" in length)

1. Sauté green onions and mushrooms in one cup of olive oil until clear or limp.

2. Add crabmeat, pimento and sherry and allow to marinate until warm throughout.

3. Season with salt to taste.

4. Place three toast points per serving on plate with wide ends of toast meeting in the middle and points facing out as a star.

5. Mound crabmeat on top of toast.

6. Sprinkle lightly with parsley.

7. Garnish with sprig of parsley.

Bon Ton Café
401 Magazine Street

"The crab that walks too far falls in the pot."
Italian proverb

Egg Dolores

1822 Bougainvillea House is located deep in the French Quarter on a quite street and proprietors, Greg and Pat Kahn, seek to make their charming bed and breakfast reminiscent of a simpler time while bringing New Orleans culture to their lovely inn. Rooms decorated with antiques, free off-street parking, tropical courtyard and impeccable service are what you can expect when staying at Bougainvillea House. It is within walking distance to all of the famed French Quarter landmarks, the streetcar line to the Garden District and musical Frenchmen Street.

8 large eggs
1 tsp butter
½ C. sliced fresh mushroom caps
½ C. sliced fresh green onions, including the green tops
½ C. fresh red tomatoes, diced
salt to taste
pepper to taste

1. Break open the eggs into a blender.

2. Add butter to non-stick frying pan and heat on medium heat until the butter is melted.

3. Pour egg mixture in frying pan and stir slowly as eggs begin to cook.

4. Add mushrooms and continue stirring.

5. Add onions and continue stirring.

6. Add tomatoes just as eggs finish cooking and are still moist. Stir. (Do not overcook.)

7. Remove from pan and plate with springs of parsley.

Bougainvillea House
924 Governor Nicholls Street

"When I was hungry you gave me something to eat, and when I was thirsty, you gave me something to drink. When I was a stranger, you welcomed me."
Matthew 25:35

Crawfish Ravigote

One of the first restaurants up and running after Hurricane Katrina, patrons were served a special post-storm menu and ate on paper plates with plastic silverware due to lack of personnel and water issues. Diners in those post-Katrina days remarked that New Orleans food had never tasted so good. Years after the storm, Bourbon House has gone back to its white linen tablecloths and silver, but the food still tastes remarkable.

½ C. homemade mayonnaise
¼ C. Creole mustard
½ Tbsp capers, chopped
¾ tsp prepared horseradish
hard-boiled egg, chopped
2 green onions (green parts only), thinly sliced
1 lb. crawfish tail meat, cooked
¼ C. olive oil
2 Tbsp cane vinegar
head green leaf lettuce, sliced into very thin ribbons
carrot, julienne
¼ of small head purple cabbage, sliced thin
salt to taste
fresh ground pepper to taste

1. Fold together the mayonnaise, Creole mustard, capers, horseradish and half of both the chopped egg and green onion in a non-reactive bowl.

2. Adjust seasoning with salt and fresh ground pepper to taste.

3. Season crawfish tails with salt and fresh ground pepper.

4. Gently fold in the ravigote dressing.

5. Blend together the oil and vinegar and season to taste with salt and fresh ground pepper.

6. Toss the lettuce, carrots and cabbage with the vinaigrette.

7. To serve divide the salad onto chilled serving plates. Top each with about 4 ounces of the crawfish ravigote.

8. Garnish with the remaining chopped egg and thinly sliced green onions.

Bourbon House
144 Bourbon Street

"When I get away from home for too long I start to get crazy, so I need to get back, ... We have to get back just to get our feet in the mud, in that crawfish juice, or something."
George Porter

Bananas Foster

Home of the original Bananas Foster, Brennan's has been a culinary phenomenon since 1946. Many of New Orleans quintessential dishes have first been served in Brennan's kitchen, including Eggs Hussard, Crepes Fitzgerald, and Redfish with Lump Crabmeat Jaime. Jazz brunch is always a favorite of travelers to the Crescent City. Located on Royal in the heart of the French Quarter, Brennan's is a New Orleans dining tradition.

¼ C. (½ stick) butter
1 C. brown sugar
½ tsp cinnamon
¼ C. banana liqueur
4 bananas, cut in half lengthwise, then halved
¼ C. dark rum
4 scoops vanilla ice cream

1. Combine the butter, sugar, and cinnamon in a flambé pan or skillet.

2. Place the pan over low heat either on an alcohol burner or on top of the stove, and cook, stirring, until the sugar dissolves.

3. Stir in the banana liqueur, then place the bananas in the pan.

4. When the banana sections soften and begin to brown, carefully add the rum.

5. Continue to cook the sauce until the rum is hot, then tip the pan slightly to ignite the rum.

6. When the flames subside, lift the bananas out of the pan and place four pieces over each portion of ice cream.

7. Generously spoon warm sauce over the top of the ice cream and serve immediately.

Brennan's
417 Royal Street

"Happiness is life served up with a scoop of acceptance, a topping of tolerance and sprinkles of hope, although chocolate sprinkles also work."
Robert Brault

The Orange Blossom

Café Amelie is the epitome of French Quarter style with a their 150-year-old Princess of Monaco courtyard that is magical to sit in on a quite summer night. Large oak trees, a fountain and occasional live music set the stage for a romantic evening. Creative dishes like local satsuma pepper-glazed jumbo shrimp, fresh salads and traditional desserts complete your evening. Try the Amelie, their signature cocktail reminiscent of a mojito with Café Amelie's signature touch.

5 oz. Prosecco *¾ oz. St. Germaine elderflower liqueur* *Dash of Fee Brothers orange bitters* *Ribbon of orange zest*	**1.** Pour Prosecco into a flute. **2.** Add the elderflower liqueur. **3.** Finish with a dash of orange bitters. **4.** Garnish with a "ribbon" (long, curling piece) of orange zest.

Café Amelie
912 Royal Street

"In the spring of 1988, I returned to New Orleans, and as soon as I smelled the air, I knew I was home. It was rich, almost sweet, like the scent of jasmine and roses around our old courtyard. I walked the streets, savoring that long lost perfume."
Anne Rice, Interview With the Vampire

63

Dijon Crusted Rack of Lamb with Arugula Pesto Sauce

Named after the 19th century French Impressionist, Hilaire Germain Edgar Degas, who visited New Orleans in 1872, Café Degas is an homage to restaurateur Jacques Soulas' homeland and is reminiscent of a French bistro, with good food, great service and an inspired wine list. Specialties include La Grantinée d'oignon (onion soup), La Salade Niçoise au Thon Poëlé (Degas' version of Niçoise salad) and their pizza is delicious.

Mustard Paste:
1 pinch fresh thyme
1 pinch salt
1 pinch pepper
1 Tbsp Dijon mustard
1 Tbsp Creole mustard
3 Tbsp bread crumbs
1 Tbsp butter

Arugula Pesto:
2 oz. arugula
1 tsp minced garlic
1 Tbsp pine nuts
1 tsp lemon juice
3 Tbsp olive oil

Rack of Lamb:
1 lamb rack (8 chops)
2 Tbsp 80/20 oil (80% olive oil, 20% soy oil)

Mustard Paste:
1. Mix all ingredients in a bowl into a paste.

Arugula Pesto:
1. Place all ingredients except for the oil into a blender on puree setting.
2. As the ingredients blend, add the oil slowly into the mix until thoroughly blended.
3. Spoon the pesto over the rack before serving.

Rack of Lamb:
1. Heat oil in a large sauté pan. When very hot, add the un-crusted rack of lamb and sear one minute on each side.
2. Remove the rack and spread the Mustard Paste on the meat side of the rack, then place rack in a baking pan and place in hot oven for fifteen minutes.
3. After fifteen minutes, put pan under broiler for three minutes to add crispness to the crust.
4. Remove from oven and let rest.
5. After a few minutes resting, cut into chops and spoon the Arugula Pesto on top.

Café Degas
3127 Esplanade Avenue

"Damn, and just when I was starting to get it!"
Edgar Degas

Beignets

French market doughnuts are a tourist magnet, but locals still appreciate the sugary pillows of dough that make Café du Monde a French Quarter destination. They only serve coffee, beignets, milk and orange juice, but the line is still out the door at this twenty-four hour, open-air cafe. For faster service, pick up your order at the "to go" window and eat them alongside the Mississippi River. Take a peek at how they are made through a viewing window behind the cafe.

2 C. Café Du Monde beignet mix
7 oz. water
flour
cottonseed or vegetable oil for frying
powdered sugar

1. In a bowl, combine two cups of beignet mix with water. Be sure to measure your ingredients. You may have to add a little more or a little less water to achieve good beignet mix dough.

2. Mix the ingredients with a spoon until the beignet mix is all mixed with the water. The dough should be relatively soft, like drop biscuit dough. It should not be stiff like pie dough. Do not over-mix the dough. You will have tough beignets if you over-mix the dough.

3. Scoop the mix from the bowl onto a well-floured surface. You will need additional flour to roll the dough flat; or else, the dough will stick to your rolling pin and your hands.

4. Roll the beignet dough flat and cut into 2-inch squares using a pizza cutter.

5. From around the edges, you will have scraps of dough left over. Do not try to remix these scraps and cut them into squares. If you do this, you will get tough beignets. Just fry these pieces just the way they are.

6. Heat oil to 370°F. They use cottonseed oil at the Café Du Monde. However you may use any vegetable oil you wish.

7. Remember that the temperature of the oil will drop when you add the beignet dough to the oil. Do not add too many pieces to the oil or else the oil temperature will drop and your beignets will be fry up flat. They will not puff up. The only other reason the dough does not puff up would be if you rolled the beignet dough too flat. Try rolling the dough a little thicker.

8. Fry until golden brown.

9. Drain on paper towels then sprinkle heavily with powdered sugar.

Signature Tastes of NEW ORLEANS

Café Du Monde
Various Locations

"Come for the people. Come for the beignets."
Patricia Clarkson

Tarragon Chicken Salad

Signature Tastes of NEW ORLEANS

This nonprofit restaurant, located in the Central City neighborhood, serves as the primary training ground for students ages sixteen to twenty-two who are looking for a future in the food service industry. Café Reconcile serves soul-filled local dishes at low prices and has become the destination lunch spot for locals. We are proud to support Café Reconcile's mission by contributing a portion of the proceeds from this book to their organization.

2 C. chicken, cooked and diced
⅓ C. celery, diced
¼ C. red onion, diced
¾ C. mayonnaise
1 Tbsp fresh lemon juice
2 Tbsp fresh tarragon leaves, chopped
1 Tbsp fresh parsley leaves, chopped
salt to taste
black pepper to taste

1. Combine the chicken, celery and onions in medium bowl.

2. In a small bowl, combine mayonnaise, lemon juice, tarragon, parsley, salt and pepper.

3. Pour dressing over the chicken mixture and stir to combine.

4. Refrigerate for at least one hour.

5. Serve on a bed of fresh spinach and garnish with bacon.

Café Reconcile
1631 Oretha Castle Haley Boulevard

"Cooking is like love. It should be entered into with abandon or not at all."
Harriet Van Horne

Pecan Pie

The original location on Carrollton Street is a hangout for Loyola and Tulane students, locals and tourists, but retains its lunch counter charm. Burgers, shakes, fries and pie are their lunch staples. A chili omelet highlights breakfast, but diners can expect omelets of every description. A new location has recently opened in the French Quarter, but the Carrollton Street location can be reached by just a fun streetcar ride through the Garden District.

4 eggs
¼ tsp salt
¼ C. butter, melted
1¼ C. light corn syrup
1¼ C. brown sugar, firmly packed
1 tsp vanilla extract
unbaked 9-inch pie shell
1 C. pecans, chopped

1. Beat eggs with a wire whisk or fork.

2. Add salt, butter, syrup, sugar and vanilla; mix well.

3. Pour into pastry shell; sprinkle with pecans.

4. Bake at 350°F for forty-five to fifty minutes.

The Camellia Grill
Various locations

"You don't want no pie in the sky when you die, you want something here on the ground while you're still around."
Muhammad Ali

This restaurant family has been serving fine Italian seafood to the Crescent City for more than ninety years and has become known for its oyster loaves. They also serve up excellent seafood gumbo, fried shrimp and Italian spaghetti and meatballs. Recently they have started offering charbroiled oysters on weekends. Celebrities such as Nicole Kidman and Robert Duvall have dined at this quaint Magazine Street eatery.

Signature Tastes of NEW ORLEANS

medium onion, finely chopped
½ C. freshly chopped parsley leaves, if desired
⅓ lb. butter
4 to 6 dozen raw oysters
1 Tbsp salt
⅓ gal. milk

1. Mix everything except milk in a large pot and cook over medium heat, stirring every thirty seconds until the butter is completely melted and everything is simmered.

2. Finally, add milk and cook over medium heat until the milk starts to rise in the pot. Do not let it overflow.

Casamento's Restaurant
4330 Magazine Street

"So, have you heard about the oyster who went to a disco and pulled a mussel?"
Billy Connolly

Since 1906
CENTRAL GROCERY CO.
923
and
Deli
Italian, French, Spanish, Greek Specialties
Home of the Original Muffuletta
TRAL GRO. CO.
CRABNET

Muffuletta

Home of the original muffuletta, Central Grocery Co. makes several versions, including vegetarian. The line snakes out the door during festival season, but the sandwiches are worth the wait in this old-fashioned Italian market. Started in 1906 by Salvatore Lupo, a Sicilian immigrant, this restaurant has become a New Orleans institution. This meat lover's version of the sandwich is a delicious marriage of Italian meats and cheese, pickled vegetables and olives. Each sandwich is large enough to feed a small army, so be prepared to share.

4 medium celery ribs, finely chopped (about 1¼ C.)
1 C. drained giardiniera, finely chopped (Italian mixed, pickled vegetables)
1 C. loosely packed fresh parsley, chopped
¾ C. pitted green olives, finely chopped
¼ C. extra- virgin olive oil
¼ tsp fresh coarse ground black pepper
garlic clove, minced
loaf round soft French bread (10-inch diameter, about 1 lb.) or Italian bread, cut horizontally in half (10-inch diameter, about 1 lb.)
6 oz. thinly sliced smoked ham
6 oz. thinly sliced provolone cheese
6 oz. thinly sliced Genoa salami

1. In a medium bowl, combine celery, giardiniera, parsley, olives, olive oil, black pepper, and garlic. Set aside.

2. Remove a one-inch layer of soft center of bread from both halves to make room for the filling. On bottom half of bread, spread half of the olive mixture; top with the ham, cheese, salami, and remaining olive mixture. Replace top half of bread; press halves together.

3. Wrap sandwich tightly in plastic wrap, then in foil, and refrigerate for at least two hours or up to twenty-four hours.

4. Cut into eight wedges and serve.

Central Grocery Co.
923 Decatur Street

"Except the vine, there is no plant which bears a fruit of as great importance as the olive."
Pliny

Lemon Ice Box Pie

Since the late 1940's, this location on Annunciation Street has been the home of Clancy's Restaurant, originally owned by Ed and Betty Clancy. During their ownership, Clancy's was a neighborhood Bar and Po' Boy Restaurant similar in style to those found in nearly every New Orleans neighborhood at the time. And while Clancy's has changed hands and menu, the home-style hospitality has never changed. Today Clancy's serves classic Creole cuisine in a neighborhood bistro style.

14 graham crackers, broken
¼ C. sugar
¼ tsp salt
6 Tbsp unsalted butter, melted
2 (14 oz.) cans sweetened condensed milk
1¼ C. fresh lemon juice
2 Tbsp lemon zest, finely grated (remember to zest before you juice!)
8 large egg yolks

1. Preheat the oven to 325°F.
2. In a food processor, pulse the graham crackers with the sugar and salt until finely ground but not powdery.
3. Add the butter and pulse until the crumbs are evenly moistened.
4. Transfer to a 9-inch springform pan and press into the bottom and two-thirds up the side. Set the pan on a rimmed baking sheet.
5. In a medium bowl, whisk the condensed milk with the lemon juice.
6. In another bowl, using a handheld mixer, beat the lemon zest with the egg yolks until pale.
7. Beat in the condensed milk mixture until smooth.
8. Pour the filling into the crust.
9. Bake the pie for twenty-five minutes, until the center jiggles slightly and the edges are set.
10. Transfer the pan to a rack; let cool for one hour.
11. Loosely cover the pan with plastic wrap and freeze the pie for at least six hours.
12. Wrap a warm, damp kitchen towel around the side of the springform pan to release the pie; remove the ring.
13. Using a hot knife, slice the pie, transfer to plates and serve.

Clancy's Restaurant
6100 Annunciation Street

"Pie is the food of the heroic. No pie eating nation can ever be vanquished."
NY Times

Cochon Dirty Rice

Chef Donald Link is serving up Cajun Southern cooking at this fun restaurant a little off the beaten path. Using locally sourced pork, fresh seafood and produce, Link focuses on traditional Cajun country meals. A rustic setting and classic bayou cuisine make for a memorable evening. Visit Cochon Butcher shop next door for delicious meats, sandwiches and wine and beer for you to take home.

4 Tbsp lard or vegetable oil
eggplant, medium dice
¼ lb. bacon, small dice
½ lb. chicken hearts and gizzards, ground
¼ lb. pork shoulder, ground
½ C. onion, small dice
½ C. poblano pepper, small dice
½ C. celery, small dice
1 Tbsp garlic, mince
2 tsp cayenne pepper, ground
3 tsp salt
2 tsp freshly ground black pepper
1 tsp thyme, dried
2 bay leaves
2¼ C. chicken stock
¼ lb. chicken liver, ground
1 C. Louisiana rice
2 green onions, sliced
1 Tbsp parsley, chopped
dash of hot sauce, Louisiana style

1. In a large skillet with a tight-fitting lid, heat lard until shimmering.
2. Add eggplant and sauté until brown; transfer to paper towel to drain. Reserve.
3. Add bacon, hearts, gizzards and pork to skillet. Brown thoroughly over high heat.
4. Stir in onions, peppers and celery, scraping pan, until onions are golden.
5. Add garlic and cook for four to five minutes, until soft.
6. Add cayenne pepper, salt, freshly ground black pepper, thyme and bay leaves and toast lightly.
7. Add chicken stock. Scrape pan; bring to simmer.
8. Add browned eggplant, then chicken livers. Return to simmer.
9. Add rice and stir to combine.
10. Increase heat to high and bring to boil. Reduce heat and simmer, covered, until all liquid is absorbed, approximately twenty minutes. Remove from heat and rest, covered, for ten minutes.
11. Turn rice out onto serving dish.
12. Adjust seasoning.
13. Add green onions, parsley and hot sauce. Fluff with a fork and serve.

Cochon Restaurant
930 Tchoupitoulas Street

"I love to cook comfort food. I'll make fish and vegetables or meat and vegetables and potatoes or rice. The ritual of it is fun for me, and the creativity of it."
Reese Witherspoon

Bread Pudding Soufflé with Whiskey Sauce

The staff at Commander's Palace put on a delicately choreographed food ballet when it comes to weekend brunch. From the chef who prepares carefully chosen seasonal ingredients, to the waiters who dance around the dining room as if on toe shoes, accompanied by the live jazz band, brunch at Commander's is as much ceremony as substance. You will leave full and content on a Sunday afternoon. During the week, their lunch specials (especially the cocktails) and their dinner menu make this a great place to celebrate any occasion.

Bread Pudding:
¾ C. sugar
1 tsp ground cinnamon
pinch of nutmeg
3 medium eggs
1 C. heavy cream
1 tsp vanilla extract
5 C. New Orleans French bread, 1-inch cubed (New Orleans French bread is very light and tender. If substitute bread is used that is too dense, it will soak up all the custard and the recipe won't work.)
⅓ C. raisins

Meringue:
9 medium egg whites
¾ C. sugar
¼ tsp cream of tartar

Whiskey Sauce:
1 C. heavy cream
½ Tbsp cornstarch
1 Tbsp water
3 Tbsp sugar
¼ C. bourbon

Bread Pudding:
1. Preheat oven to 350°F.
2. Grease 8-inch square baking pan.
3. Combine sugar, cinnamon, and nutmeg in a large bowl.
4. Beat in the eggs until smooth and then work in the heavy cream.
5. Add the vanilla, then the bread cubes.
6. Allow bread to soak up custard.
7. Place the raisins in the greased pan.
8. Top with the egg mixture, which prevents the raisins from burning.
9. Bake for approximately twenty-five to thirty minutes or until the pudding has a golden brown color and is firm to the touch. If a toothpick inserted in the pudding comes out clean, it is done. The mixture of pudding should be nice and moist, not runny or dry.
10. Cool to room temperature.

Whiskey Sauce:
1. Place the cream in a small saucepan over medium heat, and bring to a boil.
2. Whisk cornstarch and water together, and add to cream while whisking.
3. Bring to a boil. Whisk and let simmer for a few seconds, taking care not to burn the mixture on the bottom. Remove from heat.
4. Stir in the sugar and the bourbon.
5. Taste to make sure the sauce has a thick consistency, a sufficiently sweet taste, and a good bourbon flavor. Cool to room temperature.

Meringue:
1. Preheat oven to 350°F. Butter six 6-ounce ramekins.
2. Be certain that the bowl and the whisk are clean. The egg whites should be completely free of yolk, and they will whip better if the chill is off them. This dish needs a good, stiff meringue.
3. In a large bowl or mixer, whip egg whites and cream of tartar until foamy. Add the sugar gradually, and continue whipping until shiny and thick.
4. Test with a clean spoon. If the whites stand up stiff, like shaving cream when you pull out the spoon, the meringue is ready. Do not over-whip, or the whites will break down and the soufflé will not work.
5. In a large bowl, break half the bread pudding into pieces using your hands or a spoon.
6. Gently fold in one-quarter of the meringue, being careful not to lose the air in the whites. Add a portion of this base to each of the ramekins.
7. Place the remaining bread pudding in the bowl, break into pieces, and carefully fold in the rest of the meringue.
8. Top off the soufflés with this lighter mixture, to about 1½-inches. Smooth and shape tops with spoon into a dome over the ramekin rim.
9. Bake immediately for approximately twenty minutes or until golden brown. Serve immediately.
10. To serve: Using a spoon, poke a hole in the top of each soufflé, at the table, and pour the room temperature whiskey sauce inside the soufflé.

Red Beans and Rice

Red beans and rice is a Monday (wash day) staple in New Orleans. The dish is made from the leftover pork bones from Sunday dinner and this delicious one-pot meal could be cooked all day while the chef was scrubbing clothes. Coop's Place serves up traditional Red Beans and Rice any day of the week in its French Quarter setting. Expect to find other traditional New Orleans dishes on the menu as well.

Red Beans and Rice:
1 lb. red kidney beans
smoked ham shank
(smoked ham shank, which is pretty meaty, may be hard to find in some areas. Ham hocks can be substituted, but then add some ham or sausage to the beans as they cook.)
yellow onion, chopped
1/3 C. garlic, chopped
2 large celery ribs, chopped
large bay leaf
1 Tbsp Tabasco
2 tsp dried thyme
1 tsp dried oregano
2 tsp Bayou Blend
salt (add much less than you would to taste, as the shank or hock will add a good deal of salt to the dish)
black pepper, to taste
cooked rice
minced green onions
andouille sausage (or smoked keilbasa)

Bayou Blend:
4 parts salt
3 parts cayenne pepper
3 parts black pepper ground
3 parts granulated garlic
2 parts MSG
1 part ground cumin
1 part paprika

1. Soak beans. Beans are usually soaked for two reasons: it means they will cook a little quicker (a minor difference in timing, but it is there), and more important to help break down the oligosac-charides (the chemical that many people have difficulty digesting, which will then produce the infamous byproduct of intestinal gas).
2. Rinse and pick through the bean to remove all dirt, stones and broken or mis-formed beans.
3. For each pound beans, add ten cups hot water to a large pot; heat to boiling and let boil two to three minutes. Remove from heat, cover and set aside at least four hours and no more than eight.
4. Drain water from beans, rinse.
5. Add fresh water to cover and then add all of the ingredients, except rice, sausage and green onions to the pot.
6. Bring to a boil then reduce to a bare simmer.
7. Cook uncovered until beans are done, three to four hours. (You should stir the beans three to four times while cooking — and can even use a whisk to help create a creamer blend.)
8. Taste, correct seasonings, remove ham shank (or hocks).
9. Remove meat from shank and add to beans. If using hocks, add small pieces of smoked sausage or ham (¼ to ½ pound — depending on your taste.)
10. To serve, prepare rice.
11. Slice sausages in ½ lengthwise. Place on a broiler pan round side up (you can also grill them). Broil until skin blisters. Turn and cook the flat side until it is very done and a little charred.
12. Place rice on plate, spoon beans on top of rice, then place one or two pieces of grilled sausage on top of the beans.
13. Sprinkle with minced green onion.

Coop's Place
1109 Decatur Street

"Red beans and ricely yours."
Louis Armstrong

83

Lamb Loin with Honey Lavender Vinaigrette, Pickled Ramps, Local Greens

Chef Michael Stoltzfus and his wife Lillian Hubbard opened Coquette on the corner of Washington and Magazine in December 2008 in an 1880's Garden District house. With dining rooms on two floors, Coquette serves American food with an ever-evolving menu that focuses on local and seasonal products. Private parties can rent out the upstairs dining room and diners can expect fresh takes on traditional New Orleans ingredients.

Lamb:
6 oz. lamb loin, preferably American lamb
kosher salt, to taste
freshly ground black pepper, to taste
fresh thyme, picked and chopped, to taste

Honey Lavender Vinaigrette:
1 oz. honey
2 oz. rice wine vinegar
4 oz. olive oil, good and fruity

Pickled Ramps:
5 ramp bulbs
½ C. rice wine vinegar
½ C. granulated sugar
½ C. water

Frisée:
head frisée
olive oil
lemon juice

Lamb:
1. Season the lamb loin generously on all sides with salt, pepper, and thyme. Let sit for twenty minutes at room temperature.
2. Heat a sauté pan on high heat. Add neutral olive oil and when smoking, sear lamb loin on each side for two minutes. Let rest.

Honey Lavender Vinaigrette:
1. Combine all ingredients and mix well.

Pickled Ramps:
1. Thinly slice ramp bulbs.
2. Heat rice wine vinegar and sugar until sugar is dissolved.
3. Add water and sliced ramp bulbs.
4. Let sit for at least one day.

Frisée:
1. Clean frisée by removing all of the green top and large stems.
2. Season with good olive oil and a squeeze of fresh lemon juice.

Plating:
1. Slice lamb loin into ⅛-inch slices.
2. Dress lightly with Honey Lavender Vinaigrette and flaky sea salt.
3. Garnish each slice with three pieces of Pickled Ramps, a chive blossom, and two sprigs of dressed frisée.

Coquette Bistro Wine Bar
2800 Magazine Street

"Always remember: If you're alone in the kitchen and you drop the lamb, you can always just pick it up. Who's going to know?"
Julia Child

Seafood Orleans Omelet

Conveniently located in the heart of the French Quarter, The Court of Two Sisters has been serving up its daily Creole jazz brunch for decades. Dinner is also served and many brides turn to Court of Two Sisters for hosting their special day's events. Named for two sisters who owned a dress shop on the site, Emma and Bertha Camors lend mystery and history to this uniquely New Orleans restaurant.

Seafood Orleans Base:
3 oz. butter
½ C. red onions, julienne
½ C. red bell peppers, julienne
½ C. green bell peppers, julienne
1 Tbsp garlic, minced
½ lb. (31-35 count) shrimp, peeled and deveined
3 oz. sherry
½ lb. crawfish tails
½ lb. jumbo lump crabmeat
2 tsp Creole seasoning
1 C. heavy cream
¼ C. green onions, tops only, sliced thin
1 Tbsp parsley, chopped fine

Seafood Orleans Omelet:
1 Tbsp butter or margarine
3 eggs, beaten
pinch salt
Seafood Orleans Base

Seafood Orleans Base:
1. Heat butter in a large sauté skillet on medium heat.
2. Add red onions, both bell peppers and garlic and cook until soft.
3. Add shrimp and cook until they start to turn pink.
4. Add sherry and reduce liquid by two-thirds.
5. Add crawfish, crabmeat, Creole seasoning and cream and reduce by two-thirds.
6. Stir in green onions and parsley.
7. Set aside and keep warm.

Seafood Orleans Omelet:
1. Heat butter or margarine in an omelet skillet on medium heat.
2. Add the beaten eggs.
3. As the sides cook, using a rubber spatula, pull the firm edges toward the middle of the pan and let the egg run under and toward the edges (this will fluff the omelet).
4. When three-fourths of the way cooked, flip over and cook on the other side.
5. When cooked through, spoon a quarter of the Seafood Orleans Base onto the center of the omelet and slide the omelet over the other half.
6. Garnish with an orange slice and a parsley sprig.

The Court of Two Sisters
613 Royal Street

"Do not overcook this dish. Most seafoods...should be simply threatened with heat and then celebrated with joy."
Jeff Smith

Mussels with Red Stallion Beer

This restaurant, opened by Louisiana's first micro-brewery, serves its beer as well as delicious traditional American fare. Live jazz music nightly and local artwork adorning its walls brings New Orleans home at this lively eatery. Portions are large enough to share and this is a great stop when you crave a taste of home. The seventeen-barrel micro-brewery brews world class beer and has seasonal selections in addition to its regular favorites.

2 lb. black lip mussels (cleaned)
4 oz. Red Stallion beer (or Marzen or Vienna-style lager)
¼ C. onions, chopped
2 Tbsp garlic, chopped
4 oz. heavy cream or half and half
1 tsp parsley, chopped
2 oz. olive oil

1. Sauté olive oil, onions and garlic for two minutes.

2. Add mussels and Red Stallion beer (or like style of beer of choice).

3. Cover over and heat for six to eight minutes or until mussels begin to open.

4. Add heavy cream and reduce.

5. Add parsley.

6. Serve with Red Stallion and a warm loaf of crispy French bread.

Crescent City Brewhouse
527 Decatur Street

"Rather than worry about foods to avoid, I think of everything I can eat - lobster, mussels, crab, tomatoes."
Sarah Beeny

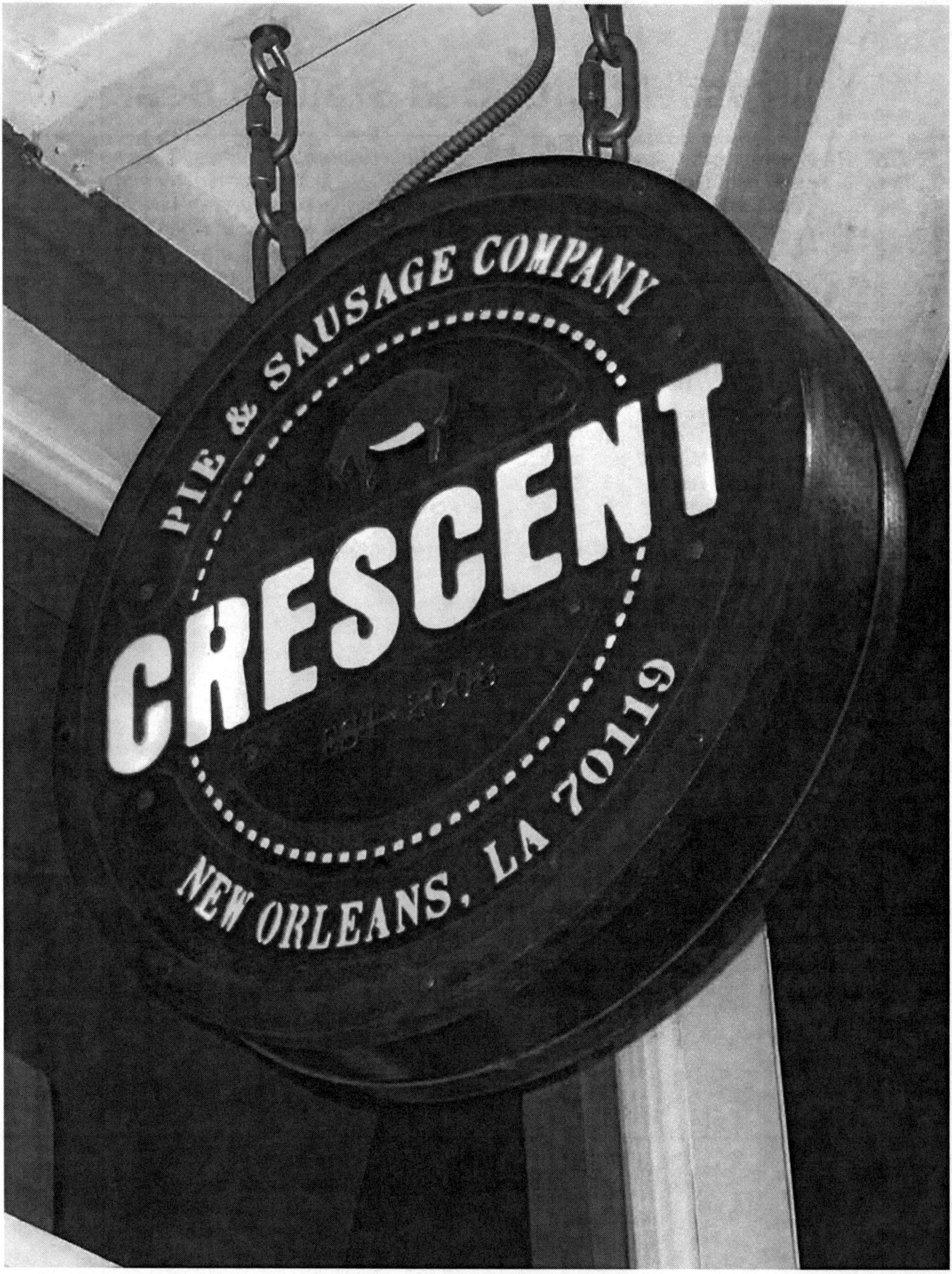
PIE & SAUSAGE COMPANY
CRESCENT
NEW ORLEANS, LA 70119

Bad Bart's Black Jambalaya

Housemade sausages, including boudin, bratwurst and Italian, pizzas and a large selection of craft beers are the specialties at this Mid-City eatery. This neighborhood restaurant offers food at affordable prices and daily lunch specials for only $10 in a rustic setting. For a real treat, try the fried mac and cheese with your meal and a slice of pie will make the meal complete.

¼ C. vegetable oil
1 lb. Louisiana smoked sausage, sliced into wedges
3 ribs celery, diced small
2 poblano peppers, diced small
1 yellow onion, diced small
½ lb. braised pork
½ lb. boneless and skinless roasted chicken thigh meat
1 (2-oz.) can black-eyed peas
4¼ C. stock (chicken, pork or beef)
2 Tbsp chopped fresh oregano
2 Tbsp chopped fresh parsley
2 Tbsp chopped fresh thyme
1 Tbsp kosher salt
1 tsp freshly ground black pepper
1 tsp granulated garlic
1 tsp cayenne pepper
2 C. parboiled rice

1. Place a 4-gallon saucepan over medium heat. Add the vegetable oil and heat.

2. Add the sausage and cook until it sizzles and curls.

3. Add the trinity (celery, peppers and onions) and cook until golden brown.

4. Add the braised pork and cook fifteen minutes, stirring somewhat frequently (every other minute or so).

5. Add the chicken, stir and cook for another ten minutes.

6. Add the black-eyed peas and cook another ten minutes.

7. Add the stock and bring to a simmer.

8. Add the fresh herbs and salt, black pepper, garlic and cayenne pepper.

9. Add the rice, bring to simmer, cover, reduce the heat to low and cook until the rice is soft, about 30 minutes.

Crescent Pie and Sausage Company
4400 Banks Street

"I do adore food. If I have any vice it's eating. If I was told I could only eat one food for the rest of my life, I could put up with sausage and mash forever."
Colin Baker

COCKTAILS

BLUE NOTE *(Kirk Estopinal & Neil Roche)* — 10
...BERRY & CUCUMBER SHRUB · SPARKLING WINE · MINT — 9

THOUSAND BLUE EYES *(Nick Detrich)*
...YATT DRY VERMOUTH, TANQUERAY GIN · ORANGE FLOWER
... BITTERMEN'S BOSTON BITTERS · LEMON — 10

FLORIDIAN VOID *(Nick Detrich)*
...RREIRA WHITE PORT · YELLOW CHARTREUSE · TRADER NICK'S
...RET FALERNUM · LIME · HONEY · ANGOSTURA BITTERS — 9

...RDEST WALK *(Turk Detrich)*
...ARD PUNT E MES VERMOUTH · PLANTATION OVERPROOF RUM ·
...IN · CLASSIC BITTER · ORANGE BITTERS — 9

LAVENDER AFFAIR *(Turk Detrich)*
...GAMMA JONGE GENEVER · DOLIN BLANC VERMOUTH · LEMON ·
...ENDER · PEYCHAUD'S BITTERS — 9

...RROW IN THE GALE *(James Ives)*
...ALO TRACE BOURBON · NARDINI MANDORLA ALMOND GRAPPA ·
...ON · GINGER · STRAWBERRY · BLACK PEPPER — 9

...NDITO *(Neil Bodenheimer)*
...RANCIO BLANCO TEQUILA · SOMBRA MEZCAL · LIME · GRAPEFRUIT PEEL
...EST XTABENTUN LIQUEUR · STRAWBERRY · ABSINTHE — 9

...NVOUS BRIDE *(James Ives)*
...OL PRIMERO PISCO · PAGES VERVEINE DU VELAY EXTRA LIQUEUR ·
...ENARINE GRENADINE · GRAPEFRUIT PEEL · SPRING LEAVE — 11

...WAS NOTHING *(Kirk Estopinal)*
...OL DE PISCO · ANTO PISCO · BITTERMAN'S CITRON SAUVAGE ·
...GRAPEFRUIT · EGG WHITE — 10

...CINNAMON ENLISS
...HONEY · PERNOD ANISE

The Benson Cocktail

Cure is attempting to reintroduce New Orleanians to a refined cocktail bar with small plates, contemporary decor and trendsetting ambiance. Named in Esquire and Travel and Leisure as one of "America's Best Cocktail Bars", Cure tries to live up to that reputation with classic cocktails and fresh ingredients for its small plates. With this cocktail you can get your daily dose of greens without knowing it.

2 slices of seedless cucumber, cut ⅓-inch thick *5 arugula leaves* *ice* *1½ oz. Silver tequila* *½ oz. fresh lime juice* *½ oz. simple syrup* *2 thick strips of lime zest* *1 oz. cava (Spanish sparkling wine)* *pinch of coarse salt*	**1.** In a cocktail shaker, muddle one slice of the cucumber. **2.** Add the arugula and gently muddle. **3.** Fill the shaker with ice and add the tequila, lime juice, simple syrup and lime zest. **4.** Shake twenty times, then strain into a chilled martini glass or coupe. **5.** Pour in the cava and add the pinch of salt. **6.** Garnish with the remaining slice of cucumber.

Cure
4905 Freret Street

"I drink to make other people more interesting."
Ernest Hemingway

Wonder Hash

This Uptown eatery recently revamped their menu and offers even more fresh, locally sourced dishes for you enjoyment. Traditional dishes get a New Orleans touch with additions like debris, Creole potato salad and grits. Try the bacon praline cinnamon sticky buns for a morning treat. In addition to their entrees, they offer a small plates menu that features interesting dishes and is great for sharing.

2 oz. amaranth
2 oz. corn
2 oz. lentils
2 oz. quinoa
2 oz. purple sticky rice
2 oz. spelt
vegetable stock
2 oz. beets
2 oz. turnips
3 oz. broccoli rabé
7 Tbsp butter
½ Tbsp sugar
2 Tbsp cane vinegar
1 tsp chopped garlic
1 oz. balsamic vinegar, reduced

1. Cook amaranth, corn, lentils, quinoa, purple sticky rice, and spelt separately in salted vegetable stock. Set aside to cool.
2. Roast beets and turnips in a 400°F oven until tender when poked with a knife. Remove from oven and cool. Peel and cut into small dice.
3. Blanch rabé in boiling salted water for fifteen seconds, then immediately plunge into ice water.
4. Melt one tablespoon butter in a skillet. Add amaranth, corn, lentils, quinoa, rice, and spelt; season with salt and pepper.
5. In another skillet, sauté beets with ½ tablespoon sugar and two tablespoons cane vinegar until beets are coated in a light syrup.
6. Melt four tablespoons butter in a sauté pan and stir constantly until browned. Add turnips, gently sautéing until tender. Toss with balsamic vinegar.
7. Melt two tablespoons butter and sauté garlic, then add rabé, cooking until just wilted.
8. To serve, mold the cooked grain mix in a coffee cup and pack tightly. Put the rabé in center of plate and unmold grain mix on top of rabé. Arrange beets and turnips around grains making sure to use some of the candy liquid and browned butter on the plate.

Dante's Kitchen
736 Dante Street

"A lot of parents ask me how to get kids to eat more vegetables. The first thing I say is that it starts from the top."
Emeril Lagasse

DAT DOG Menu

TRADITIONAL WIENERS

$5

GERMAN PORK WIENER
GERMAN BEEF WIENER

Sausages FROM HERE, THERE, & EVERYWHERE

$6

POLISH KIELBASA
(FROM POLAND)

SLOVENIAN SAUSAGE
(FROM SLOVENIA)

GERMAN SMOKED BRATWURST
(FROM GERMANY)

LOUISIANA HOT SAUSAGE
(FROM HARAHAN)

LOUISIANA SMOKED SAUSAGE
(FROM JEFFERSON PARISH)

ALLIGATOR SAUSAGE
(FROM THE BAYOU)

VEGGIE DOG (FROM OXYMORON)

CRAWFISH SAUSAGE
(FROM THE SWAMP)

Andouille Wasabi Sauce

Dat Dog is a post-Katrina addition that has come to stay. Owners Constantine Georges and Skip Murray grew up in New Orleans and after Katrina the pair took Murray's hot dog expertise, which he gained in London importing sausage from Germany, and brought it to the Crescent City. Dat Dog retains the ambiance of a globetrotting hot dog joint while giving a nod to local flavor. This is one of their wide array of unique condiments.

8 oz. andouille sausage (or smoked sausage)
4 oz. jalapeno peppers
6 oz. diced onions
1 Tbsp wasabi powder
1 oz. Cajun seasoning
4 oz. all-purpose flour
12 oz. beef broth
3 oz. yellow mustard

1. In saucepan, add three ounces vegetable oil. Add diced sausage, diced jalapenos, and diced onions. Sauté until sausage is lightly browned and onions are transparent.

2. Sprinkle wasabi powder on to mix and blend.

3. Sprinkle with Cajun seasoning and blend.

4. Add four ounces flour and blend. Cook for about three minutes until flour starts to brown slightly.

5. Add yellow mustard and mix.

6. Finally, add beef broth and stir. Allow all to cook while stirring mix until it begins to thicken. Remove from stove once sauce texture is achieved. If sauce thickens too much add tablespoon of water and reheat.

Dat Dog
5030 Freret Street

"May the dragon of life only roast your hot dogs and never burn your buns!"
Unknown

Crawfish Etoufee

1 lb. crawfish tails, packaged with fat
small to medium onion, chopped
½ bell pepper, chopped
rib celery, chopped
3 green onions, chopped
3 sprigs parsley, chopped
¾ stick butter or margarine
1 Tbsp flour or blonde roux
2 C. chicken stock
2 C. cooked rice, or 4 servings cooked pasta

1. Chop bell pepper, celery, garlic, onions, parsley and green onions.

2. Sauté all vegetables in butter over medium heal until translucent.

3. Add crawfish tails and let cook for a few minutes.

4. Add flour or roux and cook until evenly distributed.

5. Add chicken stock a little at a time until it becomes the consistency of a thick soup.

6. Add hot sauce to taste and cook for a few minutes.

7. Serve over rice or pasta.

Signature Tastes of NEW ORLEANS

Deanie's Seafood
Various Locations

"There's no place in the world like N'Awlin's, y'all. No place! I'm telling you what, I went to Deanie's last night and had those BBQ Shrimp...Make your tongue want to slap your brains out, honey. Deanie put that bib around my neck, and I'm telling you, I was in it to win it last night!"
Paula Dean

Flank Steak Bruschetta

The Delachaise is the Uptown meeting place for late-night eats and drinks. Try the duck fat fries or one of their wines from an extensive global list. Food is ordered at the bar and this hot spot is often standing room only. Affordable and lively, The Delachaise is great for a stop on any New Orleans pub crawl. Sit outside in the spring or fall when the weather allows.

Aji Sauce:
jalapeno peppers
sweet onion
green onion
cilantro
garlic
olive oil

Bruschetta:
whole flank steak
Aji Sauce
grilled ciabatta bread
aji aioli
manchego cheese

Aji Sauce:
1. Mix all ingredients together in food processor.

Bruschetta:
1. Marinate flank steak in Aji Sauce for twenty-four hours in refrigerator.

2. Grill steak on high for four minutes each side.

3. Let rest (the secret for tenderness) several hours in refrigerator.

4. Slice thin against the grain.

5. Serve over grilled ciabatta with aji aioli.

6. Finish with manchego cheese.

The Delachaise
3442 Saint Charles Avenue

"...a woman who can eat a real bruschetta is a women you can love and who can love you."
Nick Harkaway

Salmon Bouillabaisse

Boasting one of the funkiest decors in the city, near Tipitina's, Dick and Jenny's is housed in a nineteenth century bargeboard cottage. Casual dining, no reservations and an outdoor patio add to the relaxed atmosphere. Seasonally adjusted, American regional food with European touches, this reasonably priced restaurant is a favorite for family dining.

Salmon Bouillabaisse Base:
½ gal. tomatoes, crushed
2 yellow onions, diced
2 fennel bulbs, diced
1 Tbsp garlic, minced
2 bunches leeks, diced
½ celery, head, diced
½ C. anise liqueur
½ C. white wine
juice and zest of one orange
4 bay leaves
¼ tsp saffron
1 gal. salmon stock
2 Tbsp thyme, chopped
2 Tbsp rosemary, chopped
2 Tbsp basil, chopped

Rouille:
red pepper, roasted
2 garlic, cloves
¼ C. white bread slices, torn to pieces
egg yolk
1 Tbsp Dijon mustard
3 Tbsp fresh lemon juice
½ C. olive oil
¼ tsp salt
¼ tsp freshly ground black pepper

Salmon Bouillabaisse:
4 oz. salmon
1 tsp Creole seasoning
1 tsp olive oil
5 shrimp, 21/25-count
4 oz. crab meat
2 Tbsp anise liqueur
6 oz. Salmon Bouillabaisse Base
1 Tbsp butter
crostini
1 Tbsp Rouille

Salmon Bouillabaisse Base:
1. Combine first eleven ingredients in a large pan and lightly sauté.
2. Add salmon stock and bring to boil. Reduce heat to medium-low and simmer for thirty minutes.
3. Add remaining ingredients and adjust seasonings as needed.
4. Reserve warm.

Rouille:
1. In bowl of a food processor, combine first six ingredients and puree until smooth.
2. With machine running, slowly add olive oil.
3. Add salt and freshly ground black pepper. Reserve.

Salmon Bouillabaisse:
1. Season salmon with Creole seasoning.
2. In an oven-proof sauté pan, sear salmon in olive oil.
3. Transfer to a preheated 500°F oven and cook five minutes.
4. Sauté shrimp and crab. Season seafood with salt and freshly ground black pepper.
5. Deglaze pan with liqueur. Add Salmon Bouillabaisse Base and bring to rapid simmer.
6. Add butter. Adjust seasoning.
7. Transfer salmon and broth to serving bowl.
8. Garnish with Rouille coated crostini and serve.

Dick and Jenny's
4501 Tchoupitoulas Street

"Bouillabaisse is one of those classic dishes whose glory has encircled the world, and the miracle consists of this: there are as many bouillabaisses as there are good chefs or cordon bleus. Each brings to his own version his special touch."
Curnonsky

The "Perfect" Spring

John Besh and Alon Shaya have created a restaurant in the renovated historic Roosevelt Hotel that is as warm and inviting as a traditional Sunday supper in a rural Italian village. Rustic tables add to the homey atmosphere with custom brewed beers and a largely Italian wine list. Domenica Restaurant is the winner of the 2010 New Orleans CityBusiness Culinary Connoisseurs' Best Executive Chef and Best Casual Upscale Establisment awards.

2 oz. Perfect vodka ½ oz. lemongrass syrup 2 slices of cucumber 1 basil leaf homemade lime soda	**1.** In mixing glass, add cucumber, basil and lemongrass syrup. **2.** Muddle ingredients. **3.** Add Perfect vodka and shake till cold. **4.** Double strain in a chilled rocks glass. **5.** Top with lime soda. **6.** Lime soda is made with fresh lime juice, sweetener and water. **7.** Garnish with lemongrass, basil, cucumber and lime.

Domenica Restaurant
123 Baronne Street (Roosevelt Hotel)

"If you were to ask me if I'd ever had the bad luck to miss my daily cocktail, I'd have to say that I doubt it; where certain things are concerned, I plan ahead."
Luis Bunuel

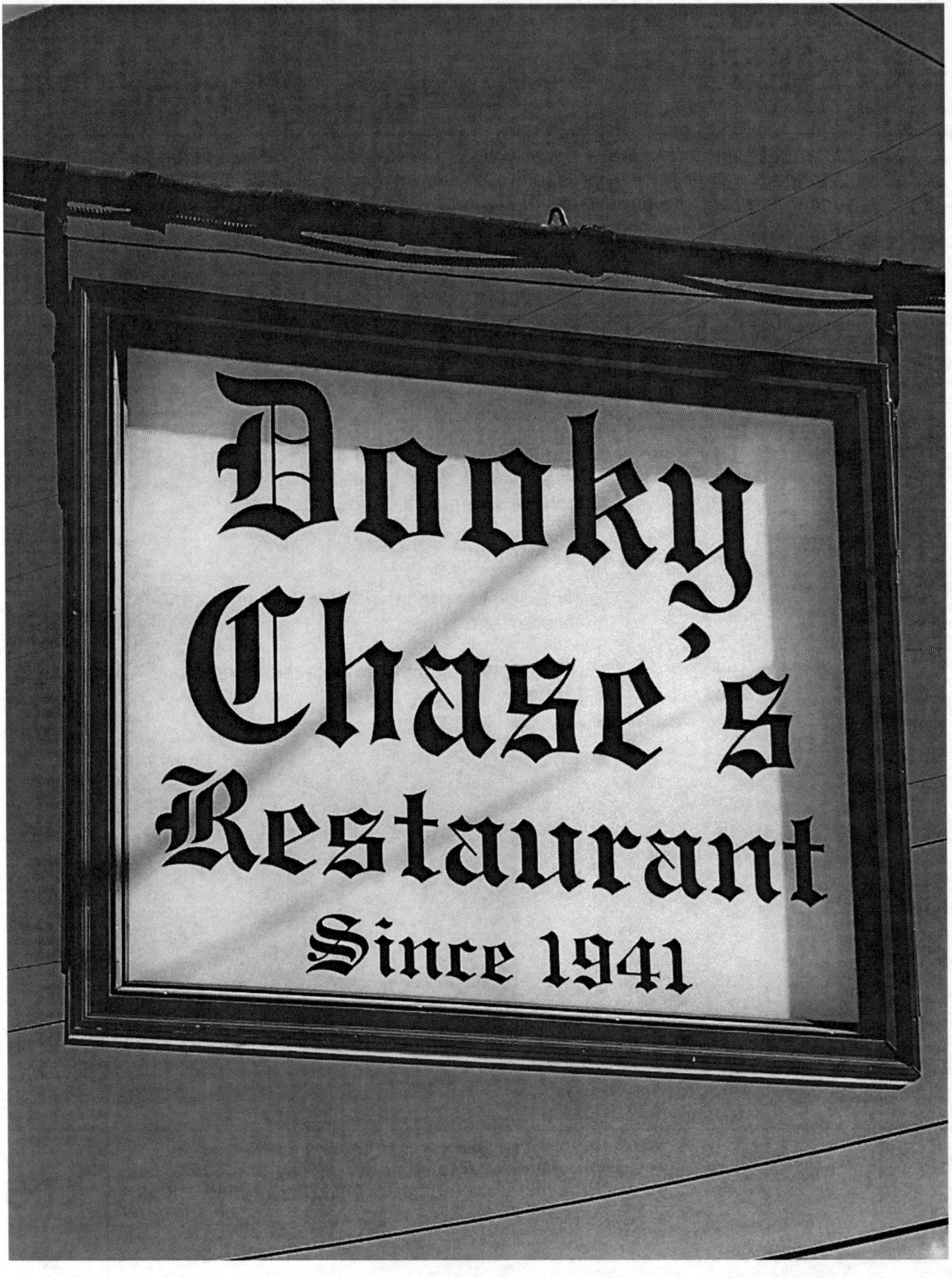
Dooky
Chase's
Restaurant
Since 1941

Gumbo Z'Herbes

Signature Tastes of NEW ORLEANS

*Considered the matron of New Orleans cooking, Leah Chase has been oper-
ating her Mid-City restaurant since 1945 and has endured neighborhood
blight, the civil rights movement and Hurricane Katrina. This landmark of
New Orleans cooking serves Creole comfort food. Gumbo Z'Herbes is tradi-
tionally served on Holy Thursday, which is the Thursday before Good Friday.
Since rebuilding after Hurricane Katrina, Dooky Chase's Restaurant is open
for lunch Tuesday through Friday and Friday night dinner.*

bunch mustard greens,
triple-washed, coarsely
chopped
bunch collard greens,
triple-washed, coarsely
chopped
bunch turnip greens,
triple-washed, coarsely
chopped
bunch watercress,
coarsely chopped
bunch beet tops,
washed, coarsely
chopped
bunch carrot tops,
washed, coarsely
chopped
½ head of lettuce,
coarsely chopped
½ head of cabbage,
coarsely chopped
bunch spinach, triple-
washed, coarsely
chopped
3 C. onions, diced
½ C. garlic, chopped
5 Tbsp flour
1 lb. smoked sausage,
smoked, 1-inch dice
1 lb. smoked ham,
1-inch dice
1 lb. spicy sausage,
1-inch dice
1 lb. brisket, 1-inch dice
1 lb. stew meat, 1-inch
dice
1 tsp thyme leaves
salt, as needed
cayenne pepper, as
needed
1 Tbsp filé powder

1. In a 12-quart pot, filled with one and one-
half gallons of water, bring greens, watercress,
tops, lettuce, cabbage, spinach, onions and garlic to a rolling boil. Reduce heat and simmer,
covered, for thirty minutes.
2. Using a slotted spoon, remove greens and
drain. Reserve cooking liquid in pot.
3. Place greens into bowl of food processor and
puree.
4. Transfer to mixing bowl and gradually blend
with flour. Reserve.
5. Place sausages, ham, stew meat and brisket
into pot with cooking liquid and bring to low
boil, cover and cook thirty minutes.
6. Add puree, thyme, salt and freshly ground
black pepper.
7. Cover and simmer, stirring occasionally until
meat is tender, approximately one hour. Add
water as needed to retain volume.
8. Add cayenne and filé powder, stir well, and
adjust seasoning as needed.
9. Ladle gumbo over steamed rice and serve.

Dooky Chase's Restaurant
2301 Orleans Avenue

"Sooner or later Southerners all come home,
not to die, but to eat gumbo."
Eugene Walter

Charbroiled Oysters

Signature Taste of NEW ORLEANS

People come from around the world to sample Drago's charbroiled bits of heaven. The original restaurant, located in Metairie, opened in 1969, offering delicious seafood and a good time to guests at a reasonable price. With a bit of garlic, butter and herbs, cooked in the shell on the grill, Drago's Oysters are special and popular. Drago's grills more than 900 dozen a day. In addition to their Metairie location, the French Quarter boasts a Drago's at the Hilton New Orleans Riverside.

8 oz. (2 sticks) soft-ened butter
2 Tbsp finely chopped garlic
1 tsp black pepper
pinch dried oregano
1½ dozen large, freshly shucked oys-ters on the half shell
¼ C. grated Parme-san and Romano cheeses, mixed
2 tsp chopped flat-leaf parsley

1. Heat a gas or charcoal grill.

2. In a medium bowl, mix butter with garlic, pepper, and oregano.

3. Place oysters on the half shell right over the hottest part of the grill.

4. Spoon enough of the seasoned butter over the oysters so that some of it will overflow into the fire and flame up a bit.

5. The oysters are ready when they puff up and get curly on the sides, about five minutes.

6. Sprinkle the grated Parmesan, Romano and the parsley on top.

7. Serve on the shells immediately with hot French bread.

Drago's Seafood Restaurant
Various Locations

"Oysters are the most tender and delicate of all seafoods. They stay in bed all day and night. They never work or take exercise, are stupendous drinkers, and wait for their meals to come to them."
Hector Bolitho

Praline Bacon

Elizabeth's Restaurant began serving this melt in your mouth bacon years before the latest sweet and salty bacon craze. Easy to prepare, this tasty treat adds a special something to breakfast. Elizabeth's Bywater neighborhood restaurant's motto is "real food, done real good" and this funky local eatery lives up to the motto. Everything is made from scratch, is carefully selected and prepared with care and creativity.

1 lb. brown sugar 1 C. pecans 5 to 6 lb. bacon, thick-cut	**1.** Mix brown sugar and pecans in food processor to a powder. **2.** Cook bacon halfway in oven heated to 350°F. **3.** Remove from oven and degrease. **4.** Sprinkle bacon lightly with praline powder, return to oven and finish cooking, rotating pan until sugar breaks. **5.** Remove from oven, and reserve. **6.** Serve four pieces per person.

Elizabeth's Restaurant
601 Gallier Street

"Bacon is the candy bar of meat"
Unknown

Rosemary Biscuits

Emeril Lagasse wasn't born in New Orleans, but the call of the Big Easy was hard to resist, especially when that call came from respected New Orleans restaurateurs, Dick and Ella Brennan. Serving as executive chef of the famed Commander's Palace restaurant, Lagasse came to love the city, its culture and its cuisine. He now has three restaurants in New Orleans, with this restaurant as the flagship. Located in the Warehouse District, Emeril's New Orleans delivers classic New Orleans food with the service you would expect from a world-class dining establishment.

1 C. all-purpose flour
1 tsp baking powder
⅛ tsp baking soda
½ tsp salt
3 Tbsp unsalted butter
½ to ¾ C. buttermilk
1 Tbsp minced, fresh rosemary

1. Sift the dry ingredients into a large mixing bowl.
2. Work the butter into the flour with your fingers or a fork until the mixture resembles coarse crumbs.
3. Add one-half cup of the buttermilk, a little at a time, using your hands, to work it in just until thoroughly incorporated and a smooth ball of dough forms.
4. Add up to additional one-fourth cup buttermilk if the mixture is too dry, being very careful not to overwork or over-handle the dough, or the biscuits will be tough.
5. On a lightly floured surface, pat the dough into a circle about 7-inches in diameter and ½-inch thick, using a 1-inch round cookie cutter, cut out twelve biscuits.
6. Place the biscuits on a large baking sheet.
7. Bake until golden on top and lightly brown on the bottom, ten to twelve minutes.
8. Serve warm.

Emeril's New Orleans
800 Tchoupitoulas Street

"I came here because the city has a tradition and is a very respected food city."
Emeril Lagasse

Peanut Butter Pie

One of the most romantic restaurants in the city, Feelings Cafe is located in the Marigny neigborhood in a historic plantation building. Dining rooms are located in both the main house and old slave quarters. Dine upstairs on the balcony overlooking the courtyard, with soft, romantic music serenading you from the piano lounge for that special date night.

12-oz. box vanilla wafers, crushed in a food processor (3 C. crumbs)
½ C. (1 stick) butter, melted
8-oz. package cream cheese, softened
½ C. peanut butter
½ of a 14-oz. condensed milk (about ½ C.)
1 C. confectioner's sugar, sifted
8 to 10 oz. Cool Whip (3 C.), more for garnish
semi-sweet chocolate shavings, for garnish
unsalted peanuts, for garnish

1. Heat oven to 350°F.
2. Place vanilla wafer crumbs in a medium bowl.
3. Pour over the melted butter and stir to combine.
4. Divide equally into two 9-inch pie tins. Press mixture onto bottom and up sides of pie dish.
5. Transfer to oven and bake until golden brown, ten to fifteen minutes. Remove to a rack to cool completely.
6. In the bowl of an electric mixer fitted with the paddle attachment combine the cream cheese, peanut butter, and condensed milk. Mix until smooth.
7. Add confectioner's sugar.
8. Using a large rubber spatula fold in three cups Cool Whip.
9. Pour mixture into cooled pie shells.
10. Decorate, as desired, with more Cool Whip. Garnish with chocolate shavings and peanuts.
11. Refrigerate or freeze until firm.

"It's like peanut butter and chocolate. Each is great, but they're better together."
Richard Whitehead

Oysters Bienville

Another of New Orleans family-run traditions, Felix's has been in operation for more than 70 years. Dine on Creole and Cajun cuisine or sample delicious oysters on the half shell from the oyster bar. Just steps away from Bourbon and Canal streets, Felix's is close to the action. Fried fish, grilled seafood, Po' Boys and even alligator are featured on their menu. Casual and unpretentious, Felix's is a fine place to catch a Saints game while in town.

Ingredients	Instructions
1 lb. chopped onion ½ lb. chopped bell pepper ¼ c. chopped parsley ¼ c. chopped green onions 2 C. chopped mushrooms 2 C. fresh raw oysters 2 lb. shrimp ½ C. flour 1 gal. cream or milk 1 C. sherry or wine 2 Tbsp white pepper ⅛ C. chicken base ⅛ C. butter	**1.** Combine all ingredients well in a saucepan. **2.** Cook for thirty minutes or until thick. **3.** Fill oyster half shells with mixture. **4.** Bake at 350°F until lightly browned.

Felix's Restaurant and Oyster Bar
739 Iberville Street

"Oysters are the usual opening to a winter breakfast....
Indeed, they are almost indispensable."
Grimod de la Reyniere

Soufflé Potatoes

The quintessential old-line New Orleans restaurant, Galatoire's Restaurant on Bourbon Street requires jackets of the gentlemen and will happily provide one if you are a bit under-dressed. Serving up French Creole cuisine with impeccable service, Galatoire's menu favorites haven't changed since 1905 and it's a good thing because diners ask for them again and again. For a real treat, order the creamed spinach and stuff the soufflé potatoes with the creamy goodness.

Béarnaise Sauce:
6 large egg yolks
2 Tbsp cold, salted butter, cut into small pieces
½ tsp. salt
pinch of cayenne pepper
1 tsp. fresh lemon juice
2 tsp. red wine vinegar
1 lb. salted butter
¼ C. tarragon-flavored vinegar
2 Tbsp dried tarragon leaves
1 Tbsp finely chopped scallion (green parts only)
1 tsp chopped curly parsley

Soufflé Potatoes:
1 gal. vegetable oil
6 Idaho potatoes, scrubbed
salt to taste
Béarnaise Sauce

Béarnaise Sauce:
1. Place the vinegar, tarragon leaves, scallions, and parsley in a small pan over medium heat.
2. Cook for five minutes or until all of the liquid has cooked out of the pan, leaving the tarragon leaves, scallions and parsley still moist. Set aside.
3. In a saucepan over low heat, melt the pound of salted butter. Remove the pan from the heat and let the butter stand briefly.
4. Skim the milk solids off the top and discard.
5. Strain the butter to remove the remaining sediment.
6. Reserve in a warm place until ready to use.
7. In a double boiler over medium heat, combine the egg yolks with the two tablespoons cold butter, salt, cayenne pepper, lemon juice and red wine vinegar.
8. Whisk the ingredients continuously until the mixture has increased in volume and achieve a consistency that coats the whisk.
9. Use a ladle to drizzle the clarified butter into the sauce while whisking slowly.
10. If the sauce appears too thick, add a few drops of cold water to achieve the proper consistency.

Soufflé Potatoes:
1. In a large, heavy bottomed pot suitable for frying, heat the oil to 325°F.
2. While the oil heats, slice the potatoes lengthwise ⅛-inch thick using a mandolin or very sharp knife. Trim the square corners from either end of the strips of potato. The result will be a long oval shape.
3. Place the potatoes into the oil, not more than two layers at a time. Overloading the pot will cause the temperature to drop. In order to maintain a consistent temperature, move the potatoes constantly with a slotted spoon.
4. Cook the potatoes for four to five minutes, until light brown. Some will form small air bubbles. This is an indication that the meat of the potato has cooked away.
5. Once the potatoes have become inflated, remove them from the hot oil and set aside to cool until just prior to serving.
6. To prepare this dish in advance, cook the potatoes until they puff and immediately remove them from the 325°F oil and lay flat on a sheet pan. Place the wax paper between the layers of potatoes.
7. When you are ready to serve the potatoes, increase (or reheat) the temperature of the oil to 375°F. Place the potatoes back into the oil and they will puff instantly. Cook for an additional thirty seconds, stirring continuously until they are golden brown on both sides and crispy enough to hold their form without deflating.
8. Remove the potatoes from the oil and drain them on paper towels.
9. Sprinkle with a pinch of salt while hot.
10. Repeat with remaining potatoes.
11. Serve immediately.

Banana Bread Pudding
with Brown Butter

Signature Tastes of NEW ORLEANS

1 lb. day-old sour-dough bread, cubed with crusts left on
5 C. milk
½ C. light, packed brown sugar
6 large eggs
2 egg yolks
1 C. sugar
1 tsp vanilla extract
1 tsp cinnamon
¼ C. honey
2 large bananas, sliced thin (about 2½ C.)

1. In a small pot, heat milk over low heat with brown sugar until steam rises off the top. Watch carefully, as milk tends to boil over when heated.

2. Meanwhile, in a medium-size bowl, whisk the eggs and the yolks with the granulated sugar.

3. When the milk is hot, slowly temper it into the egg mixture by adding one cup of the hot milk to the eggs.

4. When they are combined, slowly add the rest of the milk, whisking continuously so the eggs do not cook.

5. When the mixture is thoroughly combined, pour it over the cubed bread and let the pudding stand for thirty minutes, periodically folding the mixture to ensure even absorption of the liquid.

6. Add the vanilla extract, cinnamon, honey, and bananas to the bread mixture.

7. Pour into a 2-inch-deep pan, cover with foil, and bake at 250° F for 1 hour.

8. Turn the oven up to 400°F, then remove the foil, and crisp and brown the top for ten minutes.

9. Serve hot or cold.

Gautreau's
1728 Soniat Street

"Life is so brief that we should not glance either too far backwards or forwards...therefore study how to fix our happiness in our glass and in our plate."
Grimod de la Reynière

Shrimp Biscayne

Reminiscent of a coastal Louisiana fish camp, Grand Isle Restaurant will take you back in time to ten-cent oysters, cold beer and simple good food. Every Friday night during the summer they not only serve up great, fresh seafood, but feature jazz on the patio and fifty-five cent oysters. The freshest seafood in town, direct from the waters off of Grand Isle, Louisiana, is this restaurant's signature, but beef and poultry lovers with enjoy their cuisine as well.

5 (22/25 count) shrimp, tail on, peeled and deveined
1½ oz. olive oil, (80/20 blend of pomace and extra-virgin)
7 slices jalapeno, pickled
8 pieces garlic, slivered
1 tsp lemon zest
1 tsp house seasoning

1. In a small sauté pan add the oil.

2. Add seasoned shrimp, cook on one side and turn over and then add the garlic.

3. Finish with jalapenos and zest.

Grand Isle Restaurant
575 Convention Center Boulevard

"Show me another pleasure like dinner, which comes every day and lasts an hour."
Charles-Maurice de Talleyrand-Périgord

Signature Tastes of NEW ORLEANS

The Green Goddess is a lovely, intimate restaurant located in a quiet corner of the French Quarter on Exchange Alley. Showcasing Louisiana seafood, sausages and local produce, combined with exotic ingredients, Green Goddess recognizes New Orleans' role as one of the greatest port cities by incorporating many of the ingredients that travel up and down the Mississippi and through gulf waters. Dine alfresco on their patio when the weather permits.

Freekeh Salad:
1½ C. freekeh
olive oil
¼ C. chopped flat-leaved parsley
¼ C. chopped mint
¼ C. basil, cut chiffonade
green onions, minced
1 dash chopped rosemary, thyme, savory, fennel fronds, or filé powder (optional)
salt
barberries

Roasted Acorn Squash:
acorn squash, halved and seeds removed
salt
freshly ground black pepper
olive oil

Ajvar:
6 roasted red peppers, seeds removed
large eggplant, pricked with a fork
½ C. roasted garlic
Chili powder blend (chilpotle, ancho, and aleppo chile powders)
2 scant Tbsp olive oil

To Assemble and Serve:
toasted pistachios
smoked Spanish olive oil
Kalamata olives
Castelvetrano olives

Freekeh Salad:
1. Combine a 2:1 ratio of water to freekeh, bring to a boil, then reduce to a simmer and cook, uncovered, for about fifteen minutes. The grains should just reach tenderness, but mushiness should be avoided.
2. Strain the freekeh in a fine-meshed colander, and run chilly water over it to get closer to room temperature. Cool in the refrigerator.
3. Dress the chilled freekeh with olive oil, parsley, mint, green onions, basil, and a scant sprinkle of thyme, rosemary, savory, or fennel tops. (Filé powder can also work a little mojo accent.)
4. Lightly season with salt and stir in barberries.

Roasted Acorn Squash:
1. Preheat oven to 400°F.
2. Cut the squash in strips resembling French fries.
3. Sprinkle with salt and pepper, drizzle with oil, and roast until tender. Cool until ready to serve.

Ajvar:
1. Preheat oven to 400°F.
2. Roast the eggplant in the oven until very soft, usually around thirty-five to forty-five minutes.
3. When cool enough to handle, scrape out the flesh and discard the skin. If the eggplant seems a little wet, let it drain on a plate giving it a gentle squeeze.
4. Combine the garlic, peppers, chili powder, and eggplant flesh in a food processor. Start the machine and slowly add olive oil. Pulse until combined. (Ajvar should be thick and maintain its shape when smeared on a plate.)

Assemble and Serve:
1. Gently warm the Roasted Acorn Squash.
2. Smear the Ajvar, from 8 o'clock to 11 o'clock, in one corner of the plate.
3. Spoon the Freekeh Salad in the center of the plate and cover with two to three slices of Roasted Acorn Squash.
4. Sprinkle the salad with toasted pistachios and dress with olive oil.
5. Arrange olives and salad greens around the salad.

The Green Goddess
307 Exchange Place

"Cookery is not chemistry. It is an art. It requires instinct and taste rather than exact measurements."
Chef Marcel Boulestin

Croustillant of Roasted Foie Gras, Sauteed Langoustines, Candied Turnips and Oyster Vinaigrette

The Grill Room is known for American and continental cuisine highlighting Louisiana products served in the historic Windsor Court Hotel dining room. Murals by renowned local artist Auseklis Ozols adorn the walls and depict New Orleans at its best. Jackson Square, the French Market and a plantation countryside were chosen for these murals to showcase the beauty of New Orleans. An award-winning wine list and local jazz musicians complete the dining experience.

8 baby turnips, blanched and peeled
1 Tbsp olive oil
3 Tbsp sherry vinegar
pinch salt
1 tsp sugar
12 leaves marjoram
4 langoustines, large or gulf shrimp, large
4 braised savoy cabbage leaf, dried
4 x 80 gr. foie gras
1 Tbsp balsamic syrup
2 Tbsp finely chopped chives
pinch fleur de sel
4 oysters
2 Tbsp olive oil
juice of ½ lime
pinch salt
pinch cayenne pepper
pinch sugar

1. Cut baby turnips in half lengthways then sauté in a non-stick pan with olive oil.
2. When they are caramelized, add seasoning and sugar, then deglaze with sherry vinegar.
3. When evaporated, add the marjoram leaves.
4. Sauté the langoustine or shrimp in oil until cooked.
5. Cool and remove shell.
6. Season and keep warm.
7. Place the slices of foie gras in a hot, but not too hot, frying pan. Sear both sides until caramelized and same color as the turnips. Pour off fat.
8. Season with salt and pepper.
9. Deglaze pan with a few drops of sherry vinegar.
10. Brush a little of the balsamic vinegar over the foie gras and sprinkle with chopped chives.
11. Sprinkle a little fleur de sel over.
12. Place oysters and the ingredients in a blender and liquidize until smooth.
13. Cabbage leaves are simply braised in chicken stock and smoked bacon, then dried out in a low oven until very crisp.
14. Shellfish oil and lobster coral powder is used to enhance the dish.
15. Lay cabbage leaf on plate then six pieces of turnip.
16. Place shrimp or langoustine on top.
17. Lay a crab tuile on top, then the foie gras, followed by another crab tuile. Spoon the sauce around with a little of the shellfish oil and the coral powder, if desired.

"To be tempted and indulged by the city's most brilliant chefs. It's the dream of every one of us in love with food."
Gael Greene

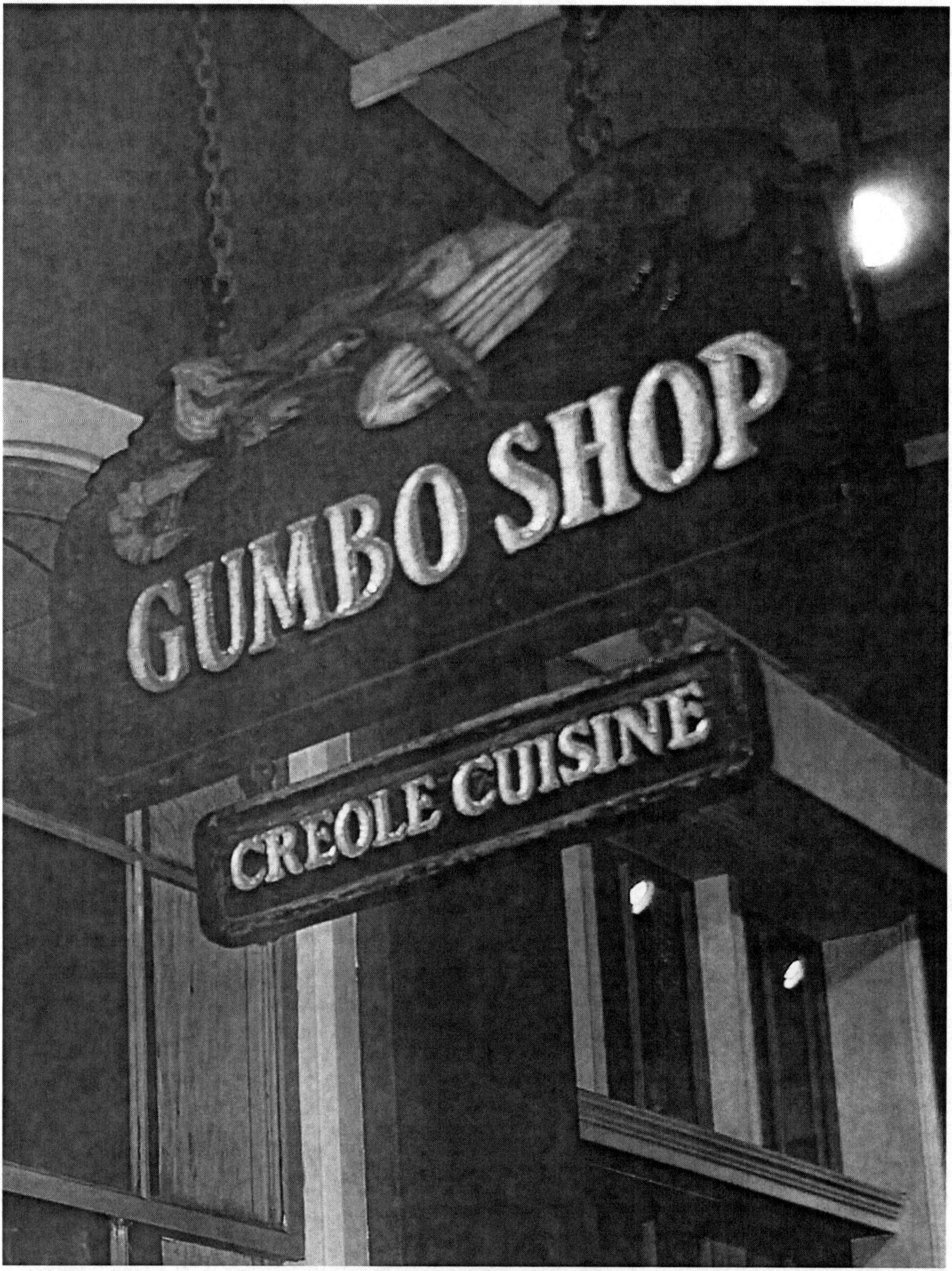
GUMBO SHOP
CREOLE CUISINE

Seafood Okra Gumbo

The local debate sometimes settles on seafood okra or chicken andouille gumbo and Gumbo Shop offers both, so diners can make their own determination on this age-old question. In addition to gumbo, Gumbo Shop offers numerous New Orleans dishes on its menu, including jambalaya, etouffee, red beans and rice, shrimp Creole and more. Located in the heart of the French Quarter, near Jackson Square, this is the perfect place for a quick, casual lunch or dinner.

2 lb. fresh or frozen shrimp, head-on, (40/50 count)
2 small blue crabs, fresh or frozen
3 qt. water
2 Tbsp cooking oil
1 qt. fresh or frozen okra, sliced into rounds
2/3 C. cooking oil
1/2 C. all-purpose flour
2 C. chopped onions
1 C. chopped green bell pepper
1/2 C. chopped celery
1 tsp garlic, finely chopped
16 oz. can chopped tomatoes
2 bay leaves
2 tsp salt, or to taste
1/2 tsp black pepper, or to taste
1/2 tsp white pepper, or to taste
1/4 tsp cayenne pepper, or to taste

1. Peel and de-vein the shrimp, and set aside, covered in the refrigerator.
2. Rinse the shrimp shells and heads, place in a non-reactive stockpot along with two quarts of water. Bring to a boil, reduce heat and simmer for thirty to forty-five minutes to make a stock. Strain, then discard the shells and heads and set the stock aside.
3. Meanwhile, wash the crabs well under running water, place in a non-reactive pot with one quart of water, bring to a boil and simmer for twenty to thirty minutes. Strain, reserving stock and crabs.
4. When the crabs are cool enough to handle, snap both claws off then break the body in half. Set aside.
5. In a heavy bottomed skillet, heat two tablespoons of oil, add the okra and sauté over medium high heat for about ten to fifteen minutes or until all the "ropiness" is gone. This step may take a little longer if fresh okra is used. (Frozen vegetables are usually plunged into boiling water and blanched before freezing, so they are partially cooked.)
6. Place the 2/3-cup oil in a large (8-quart) heavy bottomed non-reactive Dutch oven-type pot.
7. Add the flour and, over a medium high fire, make a dark brown roux.
8. As soon as the proper color is achieved, add the onions, bell pepper, celery and garlic and sauté, stirring occasionally until tender. During this process, allow the vegetables to stick to the bottom of the pan a bit, and then scrape the bottom with a metal spoon or spatula. This allows some of the natural sugars in the onions to caramelize, rendering great depth of flavor.
9. When the seasoning vegetables are tender, add the tomatoes, bay leaves and the three peppers and a little salt. Cook for about ten minutes, repeating the stick and scrape process with the tomatoes.
10. Add the sautéed okra and cook for ten more minutes.
11. Add the crab stock and half of the shrimp stock to the pot.
12. Stirring constantly, bring the pot to a boil. Lower the heat a bit, partially cover and simmer for thirty minutes, stirring occasionally.
13. If the gumbo appears too thick, add more stock to adjust.
14. Add salt to taste and adjust the pepper if desired.
15. Add the broken crabs and simmer for about ten minutes.
16. Add the peeled shrimp, return to a boil and simmer until the shrimp are firm and pink, about five minutes. Remove the pot from heat.
17. As is the case with most gumbos, this dish is best prepared either early in the day it is to be served, or even the day before, thereby allowing time for the flavors to marry.
18. When reheating, stir often and be careful to avoid overcooking the shrimp.
19. Serve in large bowls over steamed rice. This recipe will yield about six entrees or ten to twelve appetizers.

"Gumbo should grace every table."
William H. Coleman

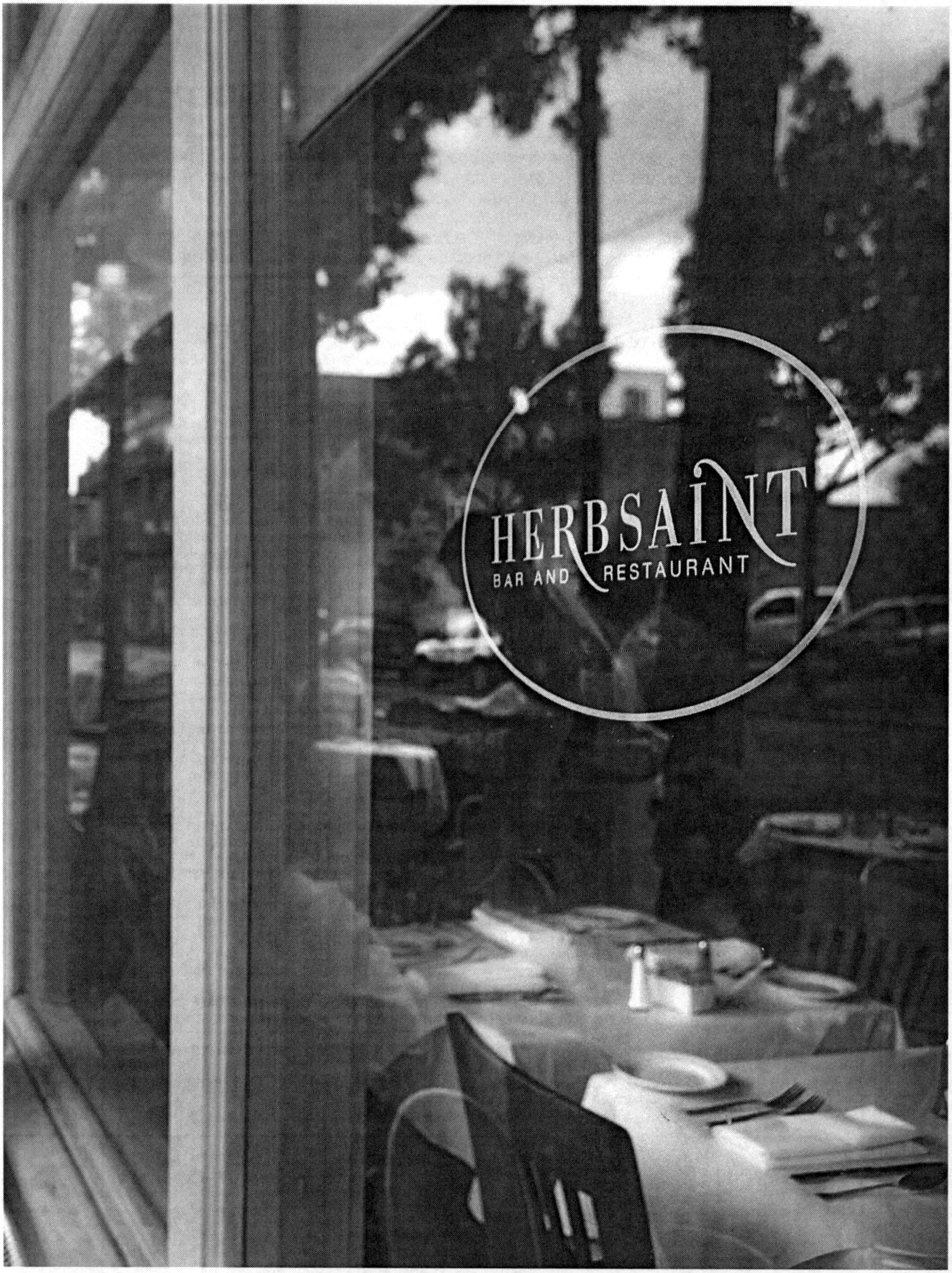
HERBSAINT
BAR AND RESTAURANT

Catfish Court-Bouillon

French and Italian inspired cuisine in a modern bistro setting right off the St. Charles streetcar line, Herbsaint is Chef Donald Link's first restaurant in New Orleans and still one of diners' favorites. Opened in 2000 with chef Susan Spicer, Herbsaint sources nearly all of its ingredients locally and a list of farms and local purveyors can be found on its website.

1 Tbsp butter
1 stalk celery, finely chopped
1 medium tomato, finely chopped
½ medium onion, finely chopped
½ bell pepper, finely chopped
1 jalapeno or serrano pepper, finely chopped
4 cloves garlic, minced
1 tsp salt
½ tsp dried thyme
¼ tsp white pepper
¼ tsp black pepper
¼ tsp paprika
½ C. dry white wine
1½ C. fish stock
1 lb. (3 to 4) catfish filets, cut into 4-inch pieces
salt to taste
freshly ground pepper to taste
½ C. flour
½ C. cornmeal, preferably white and finely ground
2 Tbsp vegetable oil or bacon fat
¼ C. chopped parsley
¼ C. chopped scallions
Juice of one lemon
5 basil leaves, coarsely torn
2 C. cooked white rice

1. Melt the butter in a large skillet over medium heat.
2. Add the celery, tomatoes, onions, bell peppers, jalapenos, garlic, salt, thyme, white pepper, black pepper, and paprika.
3. Sauté, stirring frequently, until vegetables are softened, about five minutes.
4. Add the white wine, bring to a boil, and simmer until the liquid has almost completely evaporated, seven to ten minutes.
5. Add the stock and simmer ten minutes more.
6. Remove skillet from the heat and cover to keep warm.
7. Season the catfish with salt and pepper.
8. On a plate or in a pie tin, whisk together the flour and cornmeal.
9. Dredge the filets in the flour and cornmeal mix, shaking to remove excess.
10. Heat the oil or bacon fat in a cast iron skillet over medium-high heat.
11. Sauté the fish for three minutes on the rounder, fuller side, then flip the fish and add the reserved sauce.
12. Simmer for five to eight minutes, until the fish is just cooked through.
13. Stir in the parsley, scallions, lemon juice, and basil.
14. To serve, gently remove the catfish with a spatula and set over the cooked rice. Spoon a generous amount of sauce over the catfish.

Herbsaint Bar and Restaurant
701 Saint Charles Avenue

"To eat is a necessity, to eat intelligently is an art."
La Rochefoucauld

Voodoo Shrimp with Shrimp Reduction Sauce

One of the great concert venues in New Orleans also serves some of the best Southern-inspired food in the city. House of Blues has a great place to grab a bite before an event in the two-story concert hall. A unique twist on the jazz brunch, made famous in New Orleans, is the Sunday Gospel Brunch at House of Blues. Inspiring gospel singers, a lavish buffet and good company combine for a memorable and unique way to spend a Sunday.

½ Tbsp dried basil
½ Tbsp dried oregano
cornbread
¼ tsp finely ground black pepper
¼ tsp cayenne pepper
2 Tbsp chopped tomatoes
5 Tbsp Worcester-shire sauce
1 oz. butter
2½ bay leaves
6 medium to large peeled, deveined, shrimp, with tail left on
¾ C. Blackened Voodoo Lager beer (or dark beer)
cut chives
¼ tsp shrimp base
¼ tsp chicken base
rosemary sprig for garnish
¼ C. granulated white sugar
16 oz. heavy cream

1. In a large saucepot, combine beer, bay leaves, Worcestershire sauce, black pepper, cayenne pepper, basil, oregano, shrimp and chicken bases, sugar and cream.

2. Let the mixture simmer until the mixture coats the back of spoon.

3. Season shrimp to taste and sauté in oil.

4. Ladle four ounces of the simmered sauce into the pan.

5. When the mixture begins to thicken, add one ounce of butter to the pan.

6. Add tomatoes.

7. To serve, cut a wedge of corn bread in half. Toast halves if desired. Place bottom half in a shallow serving bowl and top with shrimp and some of the sauce. Add chives. Place remaining wedge of corn bread on top and garnish with rosemary.

House of Blues
225 Decatur Street

"It you want to be real technical on the subject, while all soul food is southern food, not all southern food is 'soul.'"
Bob Jeffries

Caprese Panino

Basic Italian fare, wonderful wine list and healthy breakfasts keep customers coming back to this bright Uptown restaurant. Paninis, salads, homemade soups and meat and cheese platters adorn the menu. Grilled cheese lovers need to look no further than Il Posto to find their favorite combination of cheese and bread. Close to the Audubon Zoo and university campuses, Il Posto is the perfect stop for a light lunch or evening bite.

Basil Pesto:
¾ C. extra-virgin olive oil
¼ C. pine nuts
2 C. tightly packed basil
½ C. Parmigiano-Reggiano cheese
½ lemon, juiced

Panino:
5 oz. ciabatta rolls
Basil Pesto
fresh mozzarella thinly sliced
Roma tomatoes thinly sliced
salt, to taste
freshly ground pepper, to taste
olive oil

Basil Pesto:
1. In a food processor, coarsely chop together garlic, pine nuts and cheese.
2. Add basil, olive oil and lemon juice.
3. Pulse until basil is incorporated.
4. Store covered up to three days.

Panino:
1. Preheat panini grill to 375°F.
2. Thinly slice the dome top off the ciabatta bread, then slice ciabatta through the middle to make two equal sandwich slices.
3. Spread the bottom half of the ciabatta with Basil Pesto and cover bread with tomatoes and salt and pepper to taste.
4. Cover tomatoes with the thin sliced mozzarella.
5. Close the sandwich.
6. Drizzle olive oil on top.
7. Place on the grill for approximately three minutes.
8. Remove from grill and slice down the center and return it to the grill for another two minutes.
9. Garnish and serve.

"A man taking basil from a woman will love her always."
Sir Thomas Moore

Oysters Irene

Signature Tastes of NEW ORLEANS

Irene's is a French Quarter staple for Italian cuisine and wait times can be long because of its appeal, so reservations are recommended. Prompt service, once seated, traditional Italian fare and New Orleans desserts are part of the reason that diners return again and again. Piano music, affable staff and ample portions compliment the extensive wine list and lively crowd.

12 large oysters on the half shell
1 C. pancetta or bacon, chopped
1 red bell pepper, roasted and chopped
1 C. shredded Parmigiano-Reggiano
3 Tbsp fresh flat-leaf parsley, chopped
juice of 1 lemon

Roast Peppers:
1. Using a long-handled fork char the peppers over an open flame, turning them, for two to three minutes, or until the skins are blackened.
2. (Or broil the peppers on a rack of a broiler pan under a preheated broiler about two inches from the heat, turning them every five minutes, for fifteen to twenty-five minutes, or until the skins are blistered and charred.)
3. Transfer the peppers to a bowl and let them steam, covered, until they are cool enough to handle.
4. Keeping the peppers whole, peel them starting at the blossom end, cut off the tops, and discard the seeds.

Oysters Irene:
1. Place oven rack five inches away from the heat and set oven to broil.
2. Place oysters on a baking sheet.
3. Divide bacon equally among the oysters.
4. Transfer to the oven and broil until bacon is light brown and crispy, about three minutes.
5. Remove oysters from oven and top with red pepper and Parmigiano-Reggiano.
6. Return oysters to oven and continue broiling until cheese has browned, about two minutes.
7. Remove from the oven and transfer oysters to a platter.
8. Sprinkle platter with chopped parsley and lemon juice.
9. Serve immediately.

Irene's Cuisine
539 Saint Philip Street

"One of the very nicest things about life is the way we must regularly stop whatever it is we are doing and devote our attention to eating."
Luciano Pavarotti

Scallops with Vietnamese Greens

Chef Ian Schnoebelen dishes up award-winning contemporary American cuisine at Iris. Recently moving from Uptown to the French Quarter, Iris retains the charm and coziness of the bistro in a much larger venue. Fresh, seasonal ingredients prepared in inventive ways, set Iris apart from the competition. Beef, poultry fish and seafood all combine seamlessly to create a one-of-a-kind menu.

Signature Tastes of NEW ORLEANS

9 large sea scallops
2 qt. leafy Asian greens
1 Tbsp extra-virgin olive oil
1 tsp diced shallot
1 tsp chopped garlic
¼ C. white wine
1 C. fresh grapefruit juice
¼ lb. unsalted butter
2 whole grapefruits
salt, to taste
pepper, to taste
vegetable oil for sautéing

1. Prepare the grapefruit butter by reducing grapefruit juice in a small stainless steel sauce-pot until almost gone and thickened.
2. While maintaining heat, whisk in cold diced butter to emulsify.
3. Season to taste.
4. Hold in warm place.
5. Cut segments from whole grapefruits. Reserve.
6. Next to prepare the greens, sweat garlic and shallots in the olive oil.
7. Add greens and white wine. Cover for two minutes.
8. Season to taste. Hold.
9. While the greens are cooking, heat a large cast iron skillet until very hot.
10. Season each scallop lightly.
11. Add two tablespoons of vegetable oil and place each scallop in the pan to sear until golden brown, about three minutes.
12. Flip over briefly and place on three plates with greens.
13. Spoon on sauce and garnish with grapefruit segments.

321 North Peters Street

Iris

"Scallops are expensive, so they should be treated with some class. But then, I suppose that every creature that gives his life for our table should be treated with class."
Jeff Smith

Christmas Pudding

1 lb. dried raisins, golden raisins, dried black currants
1 oz. mixed candied lemon and orange peel, chopped
1 apple, peeled, cored and finely chopped
1 large orange, finely chopped no pith
1 large lemon, finely chopped, no pith
6 Tbsp brandy
1 bottle of Guinness beer
55 g self-raising flour, sifted
1 tsp ground mixed spices
1½ tsp ground cinnamon
4 oz. butter
4 oz. soft, dark brown sugar
4 oz. white fresh bread crumbs
1 oz. whole shelled almonds, roughly chopped
2 large, fresh eggs

1. Lightly butter a 21 pint/1.4 liter pudding basin.
2. Place the dried fruits, candied peel, apple, orange and lemon juice into a large mixing bowl.
3. Add the brandy and stir well.
4. Cover the bowl with a clean tea towel and leave to marinate for a couple of hours, preferably overnight.
5. Stir together the flour, mixed spice and cinnamon in a very large mixing bowl.
6. Add the butter, sugar, lemon and orange zest, bread-crumbs, nuts and stir again until all the ingredients are well mixed.
7. Finally add the marinated fruits and stir again.
8. Beat the eggs lightly in a small bowl then stir quickly into the dry ingredients. The mixture should have a fairly soft consistency.
9. Now is the time to gather the family and take turns in stirring, some folk put coins wrapped in tin foil in the pudding.
10. Spoon the mixture into the greased pudding basin, gently pressing the mixture down with the back of a spoon.
11. Cover with a double layer of greaseproof paper or baking parchment, then a layer of aluminum foil and tie securely with string.
12. Place the pudding in a steamer set over a saucepan of simmering water and steam the pudding for seven hours. Make sure you check the water level frequently so it never boils dry. The pudding should be a deep brown color when cooked. The pudding is not a light cake but instead is a dark, sticky and dense sponge.
13. Remove the pudding from the steamer, cool completely.
14. Remove the paper, prick the pudding with a skewer and pour in a little extra brandy. Cover with fresh greaseproof paper and retie with string.
15. Store in a cool dry place for a couple of days. Re-heat the pudding by steaming again for about an hour.
16. Serve with brandy butter, rum sauce or Bird's custard.

The Irish House
1432 Saint Charles Avenue

"A cabin with plenty of food is better than a hungry castle."
Irish Saying

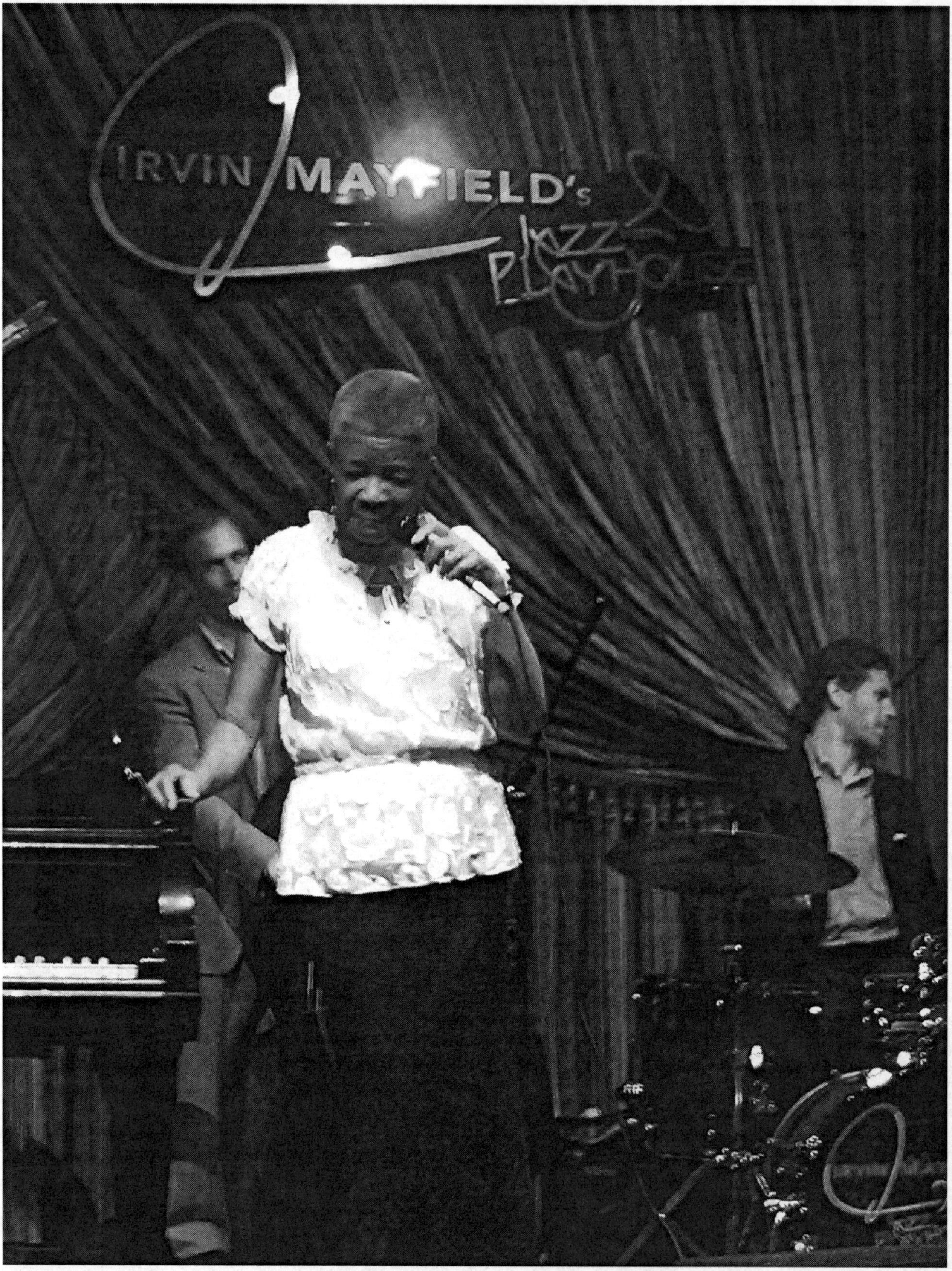
IRVIN MAYFIELD's
Jazz

The "Perfect" Parfait Provence

Jazz on Bourbon Street was once a rarity, but Grammy and Billboard award-winning trumpeter Irvin Mayfield created a renaissance with his lovely jazz club in the Royal Sonesta Hotel. Cocktails and appetizers are served in this plush, red velvet lounge reminiscent of the golden age of jazz. Jazz shows begin at 8 p.m. and burlesque is often featured late night on weekends.

1½ oz. Perfect Vodka
½ oz. Grand Marnier
¼ oz. Barenjager
½ oz. lemon juice
3 dashes lavender water

1. Shake all ingredients, except lavender water with ice.

2. Strain into prepared rocks glass over ice ball.

3. For garnish; rim rocks glass with lavender infused sugar.

4. Wrap ice ball with whole lemon spiral and place in glass.

Irvin Mayfield's Jazz Playhouse
300 Bourbon Street, (Royal Sonesta Hotel)

"A jazz musician can improvise based on his knowledge of music. He understands how things go together. For a chef, once you have that basis, that's when cuisine is truly exciting."
Charlie Trotter

Deep Dish Sweet Potato-Pecan Pie

Signature Tastes of NEW ORLEANS

Sweet Potato Layer:

1 lb. sweet potatoes (2 to 3)
1 large egg
1 Tbsp heavy cream
¼ C. brown sugar
½ tsp vanilla
¼ tsp cinnamon
⅛ tsp ground allspice
⅛ tsp ground nutmeg
pinch salt

Pecan Layer:

3 large eggs
1 C. dark corn syrup
½ C. brown sugar
4 Tbsp unsalted butter (2 oz.), melted and cooled
½ tsp vanilla extract
2 C. pecan halves, lightly toasted
dough for a 10-inch pie crust
ice cream or whipped cream, optional

Pie Shell

1. To prepare the shell, roll the pie dough and use it to line a 9-inch springform pan, molding the crust two inches up the sides.
2. Let the shell rest in the refrigerator at least fifteen minutes.
3. Preheat the oven to 425°F.
4. Line the pie shell with buttered tinfoil; fill with pie beans; blind-bake for fifteen minutes.
5. Remove foil and beans.
6. Bake five more minutes until golden.
7. Remove pie shell from oven. Cool.

Sweet Potato Layer:

1. To make the sweet potato layer, roast the potatoes at 425° F. until tender when pierced by a fork, about forty-five minutes.
2. Remove from oven, cool completely, and peel.
3. Mash the pulp in a small bowl.
4. Add the remaining ingredients, and stir to combine.

Pecan Layer:

1. To prepare the pecan layer, whisk the eggs, and then add remaining ingredients except pecans. Stir to combine.
2. Preheat the oven to 350°F.
3. To assemble the pie, spread the sweet potato layer in the cooled pie shell.
4. To toast pecans, preheat the oven to 300° F. Toast pecans on a cookie sheet until fragrant, roughly ten minutes. Watch carefully to prevent scorching.
5. Cover with the pecans.
6. Gently pour the egg-corn syrup mixture over the nuts.
7. Bake for about seventy minutes until the pie shell is golden brown and filling is almost set. The filling should wiggle very slightly. It will continue cooking—and firm up—after you remove it from the oven.
8. Serve barely warm or chilled with whipped cream or ice cream.

Jacques-Imo's Cafe
8324 Oak Street

"Dining with one's friends and beloved family is certainly one of life's primal and most innocent delights, one that is both soul-satisfying and eternal."
Julia Child

Smoked Brisket & Stuffed Jalapenos

Not your typical barbecue restaurant, The Joint serves traditional backyard barbecue with a twist. Ribs, brisket, pulled pork, sausage and chicken are all smoked to perfection and served with luscious sides. A regular on the BBQ top ten lists, The Joint recently moved to its new location on Manzant Street. Try their pecan, key lime or peanut butter pie to sweeten any day.

*18 Jalapeno peppers
½ lb. smoked brisket
1 C. shredded
cheddar cheese
4 finely chopped
green onions*

1. Cut off top end of jalapeno peppers and remove most of seeds, then set aside.

2. Dice smoked brisket.

3. Mix with shredded cheddar and green onions.

4. Stuff peppers until overflowing. (The stuffing process is easier if the brisket and cheddar mixture is near room temperature.)

5. Place stuffed peppers in pepper rack and place on the grill.

6. Cook with indirect heat using charcoal and wood chunks of your choice for about twenty to thirty minutes. Can also be done on a gas grill or in the oven, great any way.

7. Let peppers cool for ten minutes or so and enjoy with a cooling beverage.

The Joint
701 Manzant Street

A man sits with a pretty girl for an hour, it seems like a minute. He sits on a hot barbecue for a minute, it's longer than any hour. That is relativity.
Albert Einstein

Strawberry Mojito

Creole Tex-Mex style taqueria, with a creative interpretation of traditional dishes from both Louisiana and Mexican cultures. With two locations to serve hungry diners, Juan's Flying Burrito has a colorful décor, lively bar scene and some of the heartiest burritos in town. If you are planning a backyard fiesta, or an office lunch, Juan's Flying Burrito can provide take-out party platters with all the great flavors you expect from this Mexican food outpost.

Ingredients	Instructions
2 medium limes strawberries, macerated and sugared mint leaves 4 oz. Old New Orleans Crystal Rum or clear rum 3 shots bitters ice soda water	**1.** Muddle lime, strawberries and mint leaves, until it becomes of even consistency. **2.** Add ice, rum and bitters. **3.** Muddle again to break up ice. **4.** Shake and strain into glass. **5.** Fill remaining space in glass with soda water.

Juan's Flying Burrito
Various Locations

"A burrito is a delicious food item that breaks down all social barriers and leads to temporary spiritual enlightenment.
Lisi Harrison

149

Chicken, Andouille Smoked Sausage and Tasso Jambalaya

Signature Taste of NEW ORLEANS

3 Tbsp butter or margarine
4 oz. Tasso or other smoked ham, diced
4 oz. Andouille smoked sausage or any other good pure smoked pork sausage such as Polish sausage (keilbasa), diced
¾ lb. chicken, boneless, cut into bite-sized pieces
2 bay leaves
2 Tbsp Chef Paul Prudhomme's Poultry Magic, Meat Magic or Pork & Veal Magic seasoning blend
1 C. onion, chopped
1 C. celery, chopped
1 C. green bell peppers, chopped
1 Tbsp. garlic, minced
½ C. tomato sauce
1 C. tomatoes, peeled, chopped
2½ chicken stock or water
1½ rice (preferably converted)

1. Melt the butter in a 4-quart saucepan over high heat.
2. Add the andouille and tasso; cook until the meat starts to brown, about four to five minutes, stirring frequently and scraping pan bottom well.
3. Add the chicken and continue cooking until chicken is brown, about four to five minutes, stirring frequently and scraping the pan bottom as needed.
4. Stir in the bay leaves, Magic Seasoning Blend and one-half cup each of the onions, celery and bell pepper and the garlic. Cook until the vegetables start to get tender, about six to eight minutes, stirring and scraping pan bottom frequently.
5. Stir in the tomato sauce and cook about one minute, stirring often.
6. Stir in the remaining onions, celery bell pepper and the tomatoes. Add the stock and rice, mixing well.
7. Bring to a boil, stirring occasionally.
8. Reduce heat and simmer, covered, over very low heat until the rice is tender but still a bit crunchy, about thirty minutes. (If you prefer to finish this dish by baking it, once the stock and rice are added, but still a bit crunchy, bake at 350°F for about one hour.)
9. Stir well and remove bay leaves.
10. Reserve, uncovered, for five minutes.
11. To serve, arrange two heaping one-half cup mounds of rice on each serving plate for a main course; allow a heaping one-half cup for an appetizer (the recipe yields twelve appetizer servings).

K-Paul's Louisiana Kitchen
416 Chartres Street

"I don't think life is to be taken too seriously. Take it too seriously, and it'll getcha."
Paul Prudhomme

Grits and Grillades

Family owned and operated, Katie's Restaurant and Bar had its humble beginning as a corner lunch restaurant, but has grown into something more. Now this full service restaurant is open for lunch, dinner and weekend brunch. Burgers, po' boys and home-style entrees grace the menu. They also have an extensive catering menu for those parties New Orleanians love to host.

2 C. grits
¼ C. heavy cream
1 clove garlic, chopped
4 Tbsp (½ stick) unsalted butter
¼ red bell pepper, chopped
¼ yellow bell pepper, chopped
¼ green bell pepper, chopped
¼ red onion, chopped
1 tomato, cut into small cubes
1 Tbsp Creole seasoning
1 C. beef stock
1 C. veal stock
½ C. tomato sauce
½ C. red wine
½ C. olive oil
½ C. flour, plus more for dusting
4 (4-ounce) pieces baby veal, pounded $\frac{1}{16}$-inch thick

1. Cook the grits according to package directions. Keep warm.
2. Bring the cream and garlic to a boil in a stockpot until the cream rises.
3. Add the butter and whisk until creamy.
4. Add the peppers, onions, tomatoes, and Creole seasoning to the pot and simmer until soft, fifteen to twenty minutes.
5. Add the beef stock, veal stock, tomato sauce, red wine, and two cups water and bring to a boil.
6. Meanwhile, in a frying pan, whisk together the olive oil and flour and cook until it becomes dark brown to make a roux.
7. After the ingredients in the stockpot begin to boil, add the roux and whisk until the sauce thickens. Cook on low, stirring occasionally, about twenty minutes.
8. Dust the veal with flour. Pour two tablespoons olive oil in a large frying pan and sauté the veal until golden brown, about ninety seconds per side.
9. Take the veal out of the pan and cut into strips.
10. Place one-half cup grits on the bottom of a large bowl. Add the veal strips and sauce.

Katie's Restaurant and Bar
3791 Iberville Street

"You take grits for granted."
Taylor Hicks

153

Pisco Sour

This Argentinean restaurant makes a mean Pisco Sour in addition to its Argentinean steaks, pastas, chorizos and wonderful desserts. The Pisco Sour is the national drink of both Chile and Peru, but it is right at home with the cocktail culture of New Orleans. This restaurant has one of the most extensive Argentinean wine lists in town. This comfortable, rustic restaurant is located near the convention center in the Warehouse District.

1 ½ oz. Pisco (Peruvian brandy) *1 oz. house made sour mix (lime juice/powdered sugar-based simple syrup)* *1 Tbsp egg white*	**1.** Shake vigorously and strain. **2.** Garnish with a dash of cinnamon.

La Boca
857 Fulton Street

"I have a theory it is compounded of cherubs' wings, the glory of a tropical dawn, the red clouds of sunset and the fragments of lost epics of dead master."
Rudyard Kipling describing Pisco

BIBITE

GELATO

LA DIVINA
GELATERIA

PANINI

Panini

Fresh Strawberry Gelato

Artisan paninis and a lovely espresso bar may bring you into La Divina, but the made-from-scratch gelato will keep you coming back. With multiple locations in the city, a scoop of your favorite flavor is always nearby. Don't want to leave the house or hotel? La Divina will deliver their gelato right to your front door. Local flavors like Abita Turbo Dog Chocolate Sorbetto compliment traditional gelato flavors such as chocolate, lemon and strawberry.

¾ C. sugar (preferably organic)
1 Tbsp cornstarch
1 C. whole milk
¾ C. heavy whipping cream
2¼ C. sliced, hulled strawberries
2 Tbsp pomegranate juice

1. Stir sugar and cornstarch in heavy medium saucepan.

2. Whisk in milk and cream.

3. Whisk over medium heat until gelato base thickens and begins to bubble, about five minutes.

4. Pour into bowl. Cool over ice, stirring occasionally.

5. Puree strawberries in processor. Strain into gelato base.

6. Mix in pomegranate juice. Chill three hours.

7. Process in ice cream maker according to manufacturer's instructions.

8. Transfer to container.

9. Cover; freeze until firm, at least three hours and up to two days.

La Divina Gelateria
Various Locations

"Ice cream is happiness condensed."
Jessi Lane Adams

Ann's Cake

Mini
Fruit Tart

Mini
Lemon Tart

French
Vanilla Tart
with Berries

Tomato Basil Soup

This southern chain restaurant serves the best tomato soup, sandwiches and pastries just right for a quick lunch or dinner while exploring the Saint Charles avenue streetcar line. Located at the end of the line on the corner of Carrollton and Saint Charles, you can watch the cars unload passengers, flip the seats and be ready for the next load. The Croque Monsieur sandwich and salads are also spectacular.

4 C. tomatoes (8 to 10), peeled, cored and chopped, or
4 C. whole tomatoes, crushed
4 C. unsalted tomato juice
12 to 14 fresh basil leaves
1 C. whipping cream
½ C. sweet unsalted butter, softened
¼ tsp cracked black pepper
salt to taste

1. Combine tomatoes and juice in saucepan. Simmer for 30 minutes over medium low heat.

2. Cool slightly, then place in blender.

3. Add basil and process to puree. (This will have to be done in batches.)

4. Return mixture to saucepan.

5. Add butter and cream.

6. Stir over low heat until butter and cream are incorporated.

7. Stir in salt and pepper before serving.

La Madeleine
Various locations

"I feed on good soup, not beautiful language."
Moliere

Gulf Shrimp and Collard Green Stew with Popcorn Rice and Smoked Bacon

La Petite Grocery is housed in an 1800's Creole-style cottage that was home to a grocery store for more than eighty years, before being renovated into this neighborhood gourmet eatery. Executive Chef Justin Devillier was named a 2008 "Chef to Watch" by Louisiana Cookin' magazine as well as The Times-Picayne. Deviller prides himself on featuring local products, grass fed beef and Berkshire hogs in his dishes.

Shellfish Stock:
15 shrimp heads, reserve shrimp for stew
¼ C. vegetable oil
1 Tbsp tomato paste
1 C. white wine
2 qt. water
2 C. yellow onion, halved
1 C. celery, chopped
5 garlic cloves, smashed
2 bay leaves
10 black peppercorns
thyme sprig

Stew:
1 Tbsp olive oil
2 bacon slices, cut into lardons
2 C. onions, small dice
2 C. red bell pepper, small dice
¼ C. garlic, sliced
2 Tbsp. ginger, finely chopped
1 tsp cayenne pepper
2 Tbsp paprika
1 Tbsp thyme leaves, fresh
salt, as needed
12 C. shellfish stock
2 C. collard greens, sliced
2 C. okra, sliced
2 C. Creole or heirloom tomatoes, small dice
freshly ground black pepper, as needed
2 lb. shrimp, large, cleaned, deveined, halved lengthwise
1 lb. lump crab meat, picked over for shells
1½ C. Louisiana popcorn rice, cooked

Shellfish Stock:
1. In a stockpot over medium heat, caramelize shrimp heads in vegetable oil.
2. Stir in tomato paste and wine; bring to simmer and reduce by half.
3. Stir in remaining ingredients. Simmer for forty-five minutes.
4. Strain through fine mesh strainer.
5. Discard solids, reserving stock.

Stew:
1. Heat oil in a large heavy stockpot over medium heat.
2. Add bacon and cook until browned and fat is rendered.
3. Add onions and peppers; sauté until soft.
4. Add garlic and ginger. Sweat until very aromatic.
5. Add cayenne, paprika and thyme and season with salt.
6. Add shellfish stock and bring to a simmer.
7. Stir in collard greens, okra, and tomatoes and simmer over medium-low heat for forty-five minutes, until okra is tender.
8. Season stew with salt and freshly ground black pepper.
9. Stir in shrimp. Simmer until shrimp begin to curl.
10. Stir in crab meat. Simmer for two minutes. Remove pot from heat.
11. Ladle stew over two tablespoons rice and serve.

La Petite Grocery Restaurant and Bar
4238 Magazine Street

"Stew's so comforting on a rainy day."
Dodie Smith

Grey Goose L'Orange Blackberry Smash

Signature Tastes of NEW ORLEANS

Latrobe's on Royal is one of New Orleans' historic, premiere event spaces for weddings, parties and elegant affairs. Located in the heart of the French Quarter, near shopping and dining, guests will be treated to a personalized menu from their on-site chef that will accommodate any taste or group size, from small and intimate to large social events. The staff will help you plan every detail to make the event special.

1½ parts Grey Goose
L'Orange Flavored
Vodka
4 fresh blackberries
¼ part simple syrup
¼ part coconut milk
½ part lime juice

1. Place blackberries and simple syrup in the bottom of a shaker and muddle thoroughly.

2. Add Grey Goose L'Orange, coconut milk and lime juice, and fill with ice.

3. Shake vigorously, and strain into a rocks glass filled with crushed ice or a martini cocktail glass.

4. Present with fresh blackberries.

Latrobe's on Royal
403 Royal Street

"I believe that if life gives you lemons, you should make lemonade... And try to find somebody whose life has given them vodka, and have a party."
Ron White

163

MAHONY'S

POBOYS:

OYSTER REMOULADE
FRIED GREEN TOMATO & REMOULADE
ROAST BEEF & GRAVY
ROAST TURKEY & GRAVY
ROOT BEER GLAZED CHISESIS
HAM & CHEESE
COCHON DE' LAIT
PATTON'S HOT SAUSAGE
FRIED SHRIMP
FRIED OYSTERS - P&J
FRIED CATFISH
FRIED CHICKEN LIVERS
EGGPLANT PARMESAN
VEAL PARMESAN
MEATBALL PARMESAN
HAMBURGER
CHEESEBURGER
FRENCH FRIES, CHEDDAR
& ROAST BEEF GRAVY
GRILLED SHRIMP, FRIED
GREEN TOMATOES,
& REMOULADE
PEACEMAKER - FRIED
OYSTERS, BACON
& CHEDDAR CHEESE
CHEESE (CHEDDAR, SWISS,
or PROVOLONE)

SIDES:

FRIED GREEN
TOMATOS
FRIES
ONION RINGS
COLE SLAW
CREOLE POTATO
SALAD

SALADS:

WEDGE
CAESAR
GARDEN
MUFFALETTA
(ADD SHRIMP OR
OYSTER TO ANY)

DESSERTS:

SWEET POTATO
CRUNCH PIE
CHOCOLATE
CAKE W/ PEANUT
BUTTER ICING
BREAD PUDDING

6 INCH - REGULAR
12 INCH - HUNGRY
30 INCH - SUPA
MUFFALETTA
HALF or WHOLE
HOT or COLD

The Peacemaker

Mahony's is a tribute to the old neighborhood po' boy shops of New Orleans. With fresh local ingredients and family recipes, the tradition lives on at Mahony's in the Magazine Street neighborhood. Nosh on traditional ingredient po' boys including roast beef, shrimp, oyster and chicken liver. Burgers, salads, daily specials and local favorites such as Zapp's chips, Abita root beer and Elmer's Chee-wees grace the menu of this lively restaurant.

1 gal. peanut oil
2 C. all-purpose flour
4 C. cornmeal mix
1 qt. oyster meat
4 (6-inch) loaves French bread
8 slices cheddar cheese
8 slices cooked bacon

1. Heat the oil to 350°F in a large Dutch oven.

2. Combine the flour and cornmeal and mix together.

3. Toss half the oysters into the cornmeal mix and move them around, coating each oyster completely in the mix.

4. Place the oysters into hot oil and carefully move around to prevent the oysters from sticking together. Only leave the oysters in the oil for one to two minutes as they cook quickly.

5. Season, to taste, with salt immediately after cooking. Repeat with the remaining oysters.

6. Place the oysters on the French bread while they are still hot and add the sliced cheese and bacon.

Mahony's Po' Boy Shop
3454 Magazine

"Enjoy every sandwich."
Warren Zevon

Braised Domestic Lamb Shank in Guinness Stout

On a visit from New York City in the mid 1990's, partners Cristiano and Kelly dined at Martinique Bistro and love it so much...they bought it. Dishes are created using handpicked, local ingredients, produce and seafood from nearby farmers and fisherman. Once those ingredients meet the culinary maestro, Executive Chef Eric LaBouchere, they become the unique tastes of Martinique Bistro. Dine al fresco in the private courtyard.

ground fennel seed to taste *dried thyme to taste* *coarse ground pepper to taste* *kosher salt to taste* *flour, enough to coat lamb shanks* *4 domestic lamb shanks* *vegetable oil* *4 oz. slab bacon, medium slice* *4 large yellow onions, julienned* *1 large bulb of fennel, julienned* *3 (12 oz.) bottles of Guinness beer* *2 C. beef stock* *bouquet garni of fresh thyme and 2 bay leaves*	**1.** Pre-heat oven to 325°F. **2.** Season flour with ground fennel seed, dried thyme, salt and pepper to taste. **3.** Dredge lamb shanks in seasoned flour, pat off excess. **4.** Brown lamb shanks in large sauté pan with vegetable oil. Reserve lamb shanks. **5.** In a medium saucepan, brown diced bacon. **6.** Add onions and fennel, and then cook until translucent and softened. **7.** Add Guinness beef stock and bouquet garni of thyme and bay leaves. Bring to a boil. **8.** Place lamb shanks and sauce in a Dutch oven. Cover and cook in oven for four hours. **9.** When done, remove lamb shanks, and then reduce residual braising liquid until thickened.

Martinique Bistro
5908 Magazine Street

"I want all my senses engaged. Let me absorb the world's variety and uniqueness."
Maya Angelou

Asparagus Crawfish Sautéed with a Brown Butter Basil Sauce

Signature Tastes of **NEW ORLEANS**

1 Tbsp butter
½ Tbsp garlic
2 Tbsp basil
¼ C. white wine
1 oz. stock (chicken, shrimp, or vegetable)
¼ C. Louisiana crawfish tails
3 asparagus spears (per plate and blanched)
salt to taste
pepper to taste
crushed red pepper flake to taste

1. Place butter in medium sauté pan, on medium heat.

2. Heat butter until a dark brown.

3. Turn flame off and carefully add garlic, pinch of pepper, pinch of red pepper flake, then add crawfish and asparagus.

4. Toss pan and incorporate all other ingredients.

5. Deglaze with white wine and stock.

6. Add butter to pan on medium heat. Reduce liquid in pan to sauce while constantly stirring (very important to continuously stir while incorporating ingredients or sauce will separate).

7. Season to taste and enjoy!

Maximo's Italian Grill
1117 Decatur Street

"Life is too short and I'm Italian. I'd much rather eat pasta and drink wine than be a size 0"
Sophia Bush

169

Oysters Rockefeller "Deconstructed"

Combining the flavors of their home states, Mississippi and Louisiana, husband and wife chefs Slade Rushing and Allison Vines-Rushing have blended the best of both in their restaurant, MiLa, in the Renaissance Pere Marquette New Orleans Hotel. Using fresh picked produce from Lujele Farms, MiLa takes a lighter touch on French techniques, focusing more on slow reduction of juices rather than heavy, cream based sauces.

Signature Tastes of NEW ORLEANS

817 Common Street, Renaissance New Orleans Pere Marquette Hotel

MiLa

2 to 3 pieces thinly sliced bacon
1 lb. unsalted butter
3 bunches fresh spinach, de-stemmed, washed and dried
1 bunch watercress, de-stemmed, washed and dried
2 cloves garlic, peeled and crushed
salt to taste
freshly ground pepper to taste
1 lemon, thinly sliced
12 medium-sized oysters, shucked
1 stick licorice root

Bacon Chips:
1. Preheat oven to 350°F.
2. Cut bacon strips into four or five diamonds each (12 total).
3. Place on a sheet pan, and then place another sheet pan directly on top of bacon pieces.
4. Bake until brown and crisp, about ten minutes.
5. Place chips on paper towel to dry.

Spinach and Watercress Garnish:
1. Heat one-fourth pound of butter in a deep skillet over medium high heat until browning and foamy.
2. Add spinach, watercress and garlic, and season well with salt and pepper.
3. Cook until the greens are just wilted, about four minutes.
4. Let cool, then drain off butter, remove garlic, finely chop and return to pan.

Beurre Fondue:
1. Cut remaining butter into 1-inch cubes.
2. Heat two tablespoons water in a small saucepan until simmering.
3. Reduce heat and add in butter pieces, one by one, whisking constantly until mixture is smooth and thickened.
4. Turn off heat, add lemon slices and steep for about five minutes.
5. Season with salt to taste.

Assembly:
1. Heat Beurre Fondue to simmering.
2. Warm the spinach mixture and place in three neat piles on four plates.
3. Poach oysters in simmering Beurre Fondue just until they are warm and edges begin to curl slightly, about ten seconds.
4. Place an oyster on each pile of greens.
5. Pour a bit of Beurre Fondue over each oyster.
6. Top each with a bacon chip.
7. Finely grate licorice root on top and serve.

"The first man gets the oyster, the second man gets the shell."
Andrew Carnegie

171

Yogurt Salad with Cucumber

This Middle-Eastern cafe with several locations around the city serves tasty hummus and other dishes at affordable prices. A great place to grab a bite on the go, Mona's service is fast and friendly. With excellent vegetarian and vegan options, Mona's food is consistently good. The small Middle Eastern market offers hard-to-find items for your own kitchen cabinet and your forays into Middle Eastern cooking.

3 large cucumbers
2 lb. plain yogurt (regular)
1 Tbsp fresh minced garlic
1 tsp salt
1 tsp dried mint or
1 Tbsp minced fresh mint
¼ C. water

1. Peel and chop cucumbers fine.

2. Place in a medium bowl and add yogurt, garlic, salt and mint and mix.

3. Add enough water to make the ingredients soupy.

Signature Tastes of NEW ORLEANS

Mona's Cafe
Various Locations

"Animals are my friends... and I don't eat my friends."
George Bernard Shaw

Creole Tomato Sauce

Mother's Restaurant opened its doors in 1938 and has been serving the hungry workers of the city ever since. Marines adopted the restaurant during and after World War II, dubbing it the "TUN Tavern New Orleans," after the birthplace of the Marines during the Revolutionary War. Not much has changed at Mother's since it opened, with traditional recipes and long lines from dawn to dusk.

3 lbs ripe Creole tomatoes (if unavailable, use heirlooms)
¼ C. olive oil
¾ C. French shallots, diced
6 medium cloves garlic, diced
1 tsp thyme, fresh
1 tsp oregano, fresh
2 tsp white pepper
¼ C. red wine
1 tsp sugar

1. Boil whole tomatoes for one minute, then remove skins, cut in half, remove seeds and dice – should have about seven cups.

2. Heat olive oil in medium saucepan, add shallots and cook for two minutes.

3. Add garlic, thyme, oregano, basil and white pepper.

4. Sauté shallots until clear.

5. Add diced tomatoes, bring mixture to a boil, add red wine and sugar, reduce heat and simmer for forty-five minutes to one hour, or until tomatoes begin to break up.

6. Salt and pepper to taste and purée in a blender of food processor.

Mother's Restaurant
401 Poydras Street

"Everybody wants to save the earth; nobody want to help mom with the dishes."
P.J. O'Rourke

Signature Tastes of NEW ORLEANS

Mr. B's on Royal is our choice to get this quintessential New Orleans dish. The sauce is so rich you want to bathe in it, and the dish is so hands-on it requires a bib. For the uninitiated, head-on shrimp can be daunting, but with a little practice the peeling is just part of the experience. Open for lunch and dinner, as well as Sunday Jazz Brunch, Mr. B's Bistro serves up New Orleans cuisine with casual style every day of the week.

6 jumbo shrimp (12/14 count) with heads and unpeeled
½ C. Worcestershire sauce
2 Tbsp fresh lemon juice (about 2 lemons)
2 tsp ground black pepper
2 tsp cracked black pepper
2 tsp Creole seasoning
1 tsp minced garlic
1½ C. (3 sticks) cold unsalted butter, cubed
French bread as accompaniment

1. In a large skillet combine shrimp, Worcestershire, lemon juice, black peppers, Creole seasoning, and garlic and cook over moderately high heat until shrimp turn pink, about one minute on each side.

2. Reduce heat to moderate and stir in butter, a few cubes at a time, stirring constantly and adding more only when butter is melted.

3. Remove skillet from heat.

4. Place shrimp in a bowl and pour sauce over top.

5. Serve with French bread for dipping.

Mr. B's Bistro
201 Royal Street

"A gourmet who thinks of calories is like a tart who looks at her watch."
James Beard

Crabmeat Stuffing

The original, New Orleans, Cajun restaurant has been dubbed the King of Cajun dine and dance halls and serves authentic Cajun specialties set to authentic Cajun music. Located near the Riverwalk and the Convention Center, Mulate's, tempts diners to try the food and culture of the bayou in a casual, lively setting. Authentic Cajun bands nightly provide music and dancing is encouraged.

1½ sticks butter or margarine
2 medium bell peppers, chopped
3 large onions, chopped
3 stalks celery, chopped
1 tsp salt
1 tsp cayenne pepper
2 C. breadcrumbs
1 Tbsp flour
3 eggs
1 handful chopped parsley
¾ to 1 lb. claw crabmeat, picked over for shells

1. Melt butter or margarine.
2. Sauté bell peppers, onions, and celery on medium heat until translucent, approximately fifteen minutes.
3. Season with salt and cayenne pepper.
4. Mix all remaining ingredients except crabmeat.
5. Add cooked vegetable mixture. Mix well.
6. Fold in crabmeat.

Fry Or Bake:
1. Batter in egg and milk mixture.
2. Cover with breadcrumbs.
3. Fry until golden brown.

Bake:
1. Heat oven to 350°F degrees.
2. Cook approximately twenty to thirty minutes.

You also use this stuffing to stuff mushrooms, bell peppers or crabs.

Mulate's Cajun Restaurant
201 Julia Street

"When the taste changes with every bite and the last bite is as good as the first, that's Cajun."
Paul Prudhomme

Bread Pudding for a Crowd

Located just off Jackson Square, Muriel's Jackson Square serves Creole cuisine in a historic setting. Reportedly haunted, Muriel's Courtyard Bar boasts the spirit of Pierre Antoine Lepardi Jourdan, a wealthy New Orleanian who gambled away his beloved home on the site and committed suicide because of the loss. A table is always set for Mr. Jourdan, with bread and wine at the ready. For a truly spiritual experience, try Muriel's cuisine.

Bread Pudding:
21 qt. heavy whipping cream
12 C. granulated sugar
12 lb. white chocolate bits, preferably discs
96 eggs
10½ C. egg yolks
¾ C. vanilla bean marinade
21 po' boy loaves, day-old, cut to large cubes
24 qt. Rum Sauce
2 gal. Candied Pecans

Rum Sauce:
30 lb. light brown sugar
10 qt. heavy whipping cream
4 lb. unsalted butter
8 C. light corn syrup
6 C. light rum

Candied Pecans:
10 egg whites
16 C. sugar
2 gal. pecan pieces

Bread Pudding:
1. In a large saucepan, heat cream and sugar, do not boil. Remove from heat.
2. Add white chocolate and stir to melt.
3. Temper into eggs and yolks.
4. Add bread and stir to combine.
5. Transfer into six parchment-lined hotel pans. Cover with foil.
6. Bake in preheated 300°F oven with low fan for one hour.
7. Remove foil, bake for thirty minutes more. Remove from oven.
8. Pour Rum Sauce over warm pudding.
9. Top with pecans.
10. Cool slightly.
11. Cut each pan to thirty-two portions.

Rum Sauce:
1. Combine all ingredients, except rum, in a large saucepot and bring to boil. Reduce heat and simmer for fifteen minutes.
2. Remove from heat. Stir in rum.
3. Reserve.

Candied Pecans:
1. Using an electric mixer fitted with whisk attachment, whip egg whites and sugar to soft peaks.
2. Add pecans and stir by hand to coat thoroughly.
3. Transfer to parchment-lined sheet pans in single layer and bake in preheated 325°F oven for ten minutes.
4. Remove and reserve.

Muriel's Jackson Square
801 Chartres Street

"Time goes by so fast. Nothin' can outrun it. Death commences too early – almost before you're half-acquainted with life – you meet the other."
Tennessee Williams

The Pimms Cup

Nicholas Girod, mayor of New Orleans from 1812 to 1815, originally owned Napoleon House Bar and Café, a 200-year-old landmark in the French Quarter. Girod offered Napoleon use of the residence as a refuge during his exile in 1821. Although Napoleon never took Girod up on the offer, the name stuck and Napoleon House has become one of the most famous bars in America.

ice 1¼ oz. Pimm's No. 1 3 oz. lemonade 7up	**1.** Fill a tall 12 ounce glass with ice and add Pimm's No. 1 and lemonade. **2.** Top off with 7up.

Napoleon House Bar and Café
500 Chartres Steet

"History is a set of lies agreed upon."
Napoleon Bonaparte

Pralines

Learn the secrets of Louisiana traditional cooking from chefs and historians in Creole/Cajun cuisine. Housed in a renovated molasses warehouse, this cooking school offers both demonstration and hands-on classes and teaches a wide range of local classics such as jambalaya, gumbo and pralines. Conveniently located in the French Quarter, The New Orleans School of Cooking is an "only in New Orleans" experience.

Signature Tastes of NEW ORLEANS

1½ C. sugar
¾ C. light brown sugar, packed
½ C. milk
6 Tbsp butter (¾ stick)
1½ C. pecans (roasted optional)
1 Tbsp vanilla

1. To roast pecans, bake them on a sheet pan at 275°F for twenty to twenty-five minutes, until slightly browned and fragrant.

2. Combine all ingredients and bring to a soft-ball stage (238-240°F), stirring constantly. (When you place a spoonful into a glass of water and it sticks to the side.)

3. Remove from heat.

4. Stir until mixture thickens, becomes creamy and cloudy, and pecans stay suspended in mixture.

5. Spoon out on buttered waxed paper, aluminum foil or parchment paper. When using waxed paper, be sure to buffer with newspaper underneath, as hot wax will transfer to whatever is beneath. Cool.

"Candy is nature's way of making up for Mondays."
Unknown

Chicory Coffee Crème Brulees with Brown Sugar Shortbread Cookies

Signature Taste of NEW ORLEANS

Crème Brulee:
1½ heavy cream
1¼ C. whole milk
½ C. plus 3 tsp sugar
4 Tbsp instant chicory coffee or
2 Tbsp instant espresso coffee
½ tsp freshly ground black pepper
7 large egg yolks

Brown Sugar Shortbread Cookies:
½ lb. (2 sticks) plus 1 tsp unsalted butter, at room temperature
1 C. packed light brown sugar
2 C. all-purpose flour
⅛ tsp salt
1 Tbsp granulated sugar
¼ t. ground cinnamon

Crème Brulee:
1. Combine the cream, milk, one-half cup of the sugar, the coffee and pepper in a medium saucepan
2. Bring to a bare simmer over medium-high heat, stirring to dissolve the sugar and coffee. Remove from the heat.
3. In a medium bowl, whisk the egg yolks until frothy and lemon-colored, about two minutes.
4. Slowly add the hot milk mixture to the eggs, whisking constantly.
5. Strain through a fine mesh strainer into a bowl or pitcher.
6. Divide the custard among the ramekins.
7. Add enough hot water to the roasting pan to come halfway up the sides of the ramekins.
8. Bake for thirty minutes.
9. Rotate the roasting pan and bake until the custards are firm, yet still jiggle slightly when shaken, thirty to forty minutes.
10. Remove from the oven and cool.
11. Cover with plastic wrap and refrigerate until well chilled, at least four hours or overnight.
12. Sprinkle the top of each custard with one and one-half teaspoon of the remaining sugar.
13. Using a blowtorch, caramelize the sugar, (alternatively, preheat the broiler. Place the custards on a baking sheet and broil until the sugar melts and caramelizes, watching closely to avoid burning and rotating the cups as necessary, one to two minutes.)
14. Place on dessert plates and serve.

Shortbread Cookies:
1. Preheat the oven to 325°F.
2. Lightly grease a 9-inch springform pan with one teaspoon of the butter and set aside.
3. In a large bowl, using an electric mixer, cream the remaining two sticks butter.
4. Add the sugar and beat until light and fluffy.
5. Add the flour and salt and mix just until blended, being careful not to over-mix.
6. Press the dough into the bottom of the prepared pan.
7. Pierce the dough ball over with the tines of a fork, and press the edges decoratively with the flat side of the tines.
8. Combine the sugar and cinnamon in a small bowl and sprinkle lightly over the dough.
9. Bake until set and light golden brown, thirty to forty minutes.
10. Remove from the oven and release the sides of the pan.
11. Cut while warm into twelve wedges.
12. Let cool before serving, or store in an airtight container for up to three days and serve at room temperature.

NOLA Restaurant
534 Saint Louis Street

"If there was no New Orleans, America would just be a bunch of free people dying of boredom."
Judy Deck

Cajun Tea

Celebration Distillation, located on Frenchmen Street, is the oldest premium rum distillery in the United States. Using blackstrap molasses from the river plantations of Louisiana, Old New Orleans Louisiana Rum Distillery produces small batch artisan rum in a variety of ages and flavors. Artist and owner, James Michalopoulos, created his first batch in his Ninth Ward kitchen, but now his rum can be found around the country. Take a tour of the factory and see for yourself. They even serve samples.

Ingredients	Instructions
ice *1½ oz. Old New Orleans Cajun Spice Rum* *½ oz. simple syrup* *unsweetened ice tea* *lemon slice*	**1.** Fill a hi-ball glass with ice. **2.** Add Cajun Spice Rum and simple syrup. **3.** Fill will ice tea. **4.** Stir and serve with lemon slice.

"The only way I could figure they could improve upon Coca-Cola, one of life's most delightful elixirs, which studies prove will heal the sick and occasionally raise the dead, is to put rum or bourbon in it."
Lewis Grizzard

Tomato-Bleu Cheese Napoleon

Palace Cafe is housed at the foot of the French Quarter in the historic Werlein building, the former home of Werlein's Music, the nation's oldest family owned retail music chain. Serving contemporary Creole food in grand cafe style, Palace Café has won numerous awards including Wine Spectator's Award of Excellence and Best New Restaurant from Esquire magazine and USA Today.

2 slices tomato (Creole or vine ripe), ½-inch thick
1 oz. red onion, shaved
1 oz. leaf lettuce, chiffonade
2 oz. Maytag blue cheese, crumbled
1½ oz. remoulade dressing
1 crouton, cut on a bias 3-4 inches, toasted

1. Place chiffonade of lettuce on bottom of six-inch plate, in a rectangular shape about 1 to 1½ inches wide.

2. Place the crouton on the center of the plate on top of the lettuce.

3. Layer tomato, blue cheese and red onion.

4. Repeat tomato, blue cheese and red onion.

5. Ladle remoulade sauce over the napoleon perpendicular to the lettuce and serve.

Palace Café
605 Canal Street

"It's difficult to think anything but pleasant thoughts while eating a homegrown tomato."
Lewis Grizzard

Potato Po' Boy with Roast Beef Gravy

This little po' boy shop gained fame when it was one of the first restaurants in Mid-City to re-open, despite suffering six feet of water themselves. During a trip to the Crescent City, President Barrack Obama stopped to try a Parkway po' boy for himself. Now serving more than twenty-five varieties of the famed sandwich, Parkway is a great place to watch a Saints game on the patio.

Signature Tastes of NEW ORLEANS

Chuck Roast Gravy:
5 lb. chuck roast
freshly ground black pepper, as needed
1 Tbsp garlic powder
1 Tbsp onion powder
vegetable oil, as needed
6 oz. chicken broth
6 oz. beef broth
6 oz. mushroom soup
1 oz. browning and seasoning sauce

Po' Boy:
2 potatoes
oil for frying, as needed
French bread, 11-inch loaf
1 oz. mayonnaise
2 slices tomato
lettuce leaves, shredded, as needed
3 oz. pickle slices
4 oz. Chuck Roast Gravy

Gravy:
1. Rub roast with freshly ground black pepper, garlic powder and onion powder.
2. Heat oil in heavy pot or Dutch oven and sear roast until browned on all sides. Remove roast from pot and reserve.
3. Deglaze pot with chicken broth.
4. Add beef broth, mushroom soup and browning sauce.
5. Return meat to pot with accumulated juices, cover and roast in preheated 225°F oven for eight hours, until very tender.
6. Remove from oven.
7. Chill meat and gravy separately, overnight then discard fat.
8. In a pot over medium heat, warm gravy.
9. Cut three ounces meat into matchstick-size pieces and add to gravy.
10. Reserve, warm.

Po 'Boy:
1. Cut potatoes to 3/8-inch straight-cut French fries and fry in 350°F oil.
2. Slice French bread lengthwise and toast.
3. Spread with mayonnaise; add tomato, lettuce and pickles.
4. Using a slotted spoon, transfer ten ounces fried potatoes onto bottom slice of bread.
5. Pour chuck roast gravy over potatoes.
6. Top with remaining bread slice.
7. Cut in half on a 46-degree angle and serve hot.

Parkway Bakery and Tavern
538 Hagan Avenue

"It has been well said that a hungry man is more interested in four sandwiches than four freedoms."
Henry Cabot Lodge, Jr.

Pat O'Brien's
Famous Hurricane

Since 1933 and the end of prohibition, Pat O'Brien's motto has been "Have Fun!" and that is what they serve up in this iconic French Quarter haunt. This former speakeasy, Pat O'Brien's is known for its traditional French Quarter courtyard, the world famous Hurricane, dueling pianos and lively bar scene. The Hurricane was born out of shortage for scotch and whiskey. During the 1940's, in order to purchase any of these liquors, a bar owner was forced to buy up to fifty cases of rum. The Hurricane was created to reduce the over abundance of rum and when the fruity concoction was served in a glass reminiscent of a hurricane lamp, the signature drink was born.

2 oz. light rum
2 oz. dark rum
2 oz. passion fruit juice
1 oz. orange juice
½ lime, juiced
1 Tbsp simple syrup
1 Tbsp grenadine
orange slice
maraschino cherry

1. Mix rums, juices, simple syrup and grenadine in a shaker.

2. Pour over ice.

3. Garnish with orange slice and maraschino cherry.

Pat O'Brien's
718 Saint Peter Street

"The hurricane flooded me out of a lot of memorabilia, but it can't flood out the memories."
Tom Dempsey

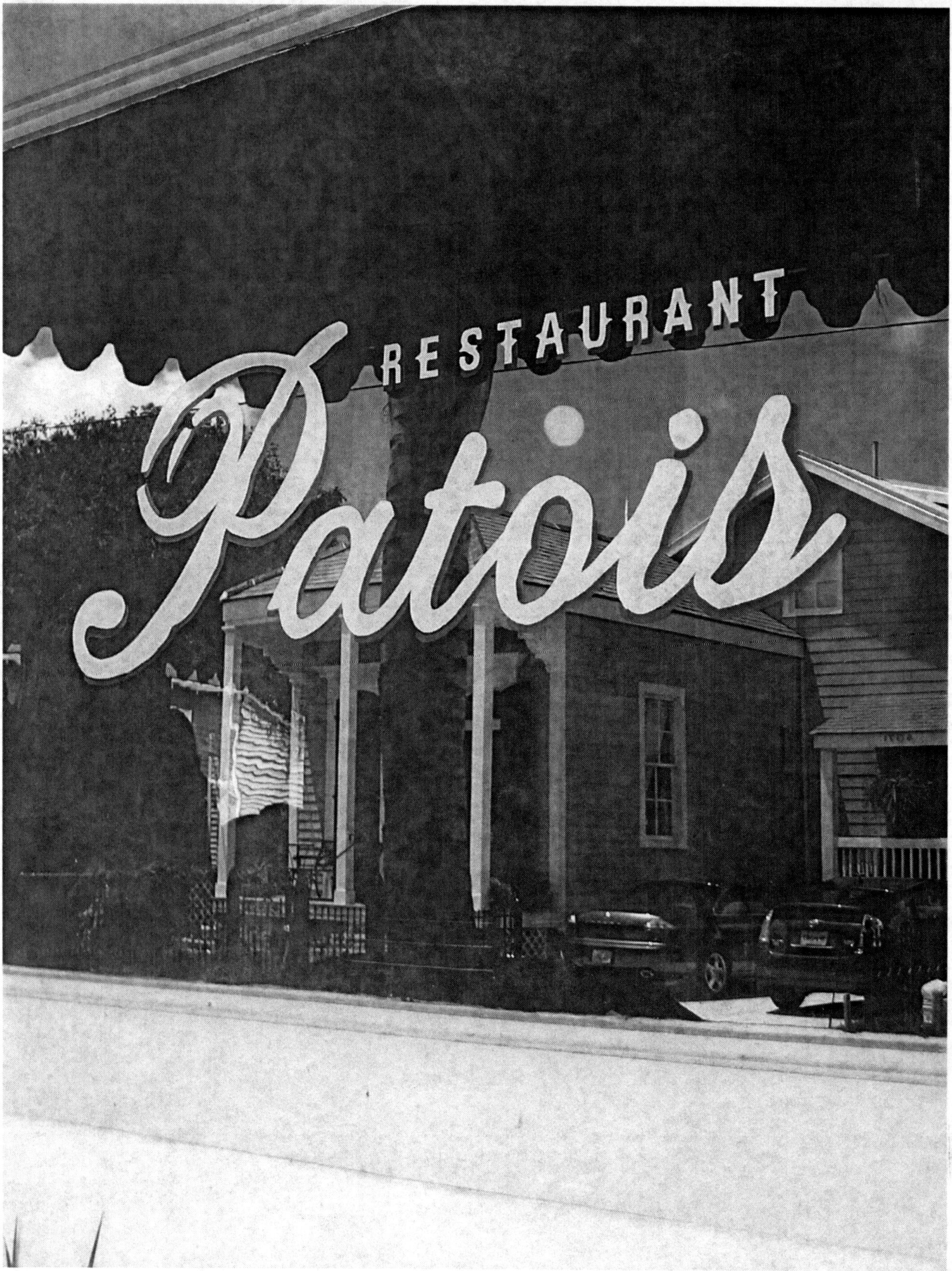
RESTAURANT
Patois

Gateau d'Sirop

Named one of the top five "Chefs to Watch" by Louisiana Cookin' Magazine, Chef Aaron Burgau opened Patois in 2007 in a quaint Uptown neighborhood with long-time friends Leon and Pierre Touzet. With family history tucked into the decor, and exceptional service, Patois serves classic French cuisine using locally sourced ingredients with a local accent. Open for lunch, dinner and Sunday brunch, Patois is located on the corner of Laurel and Webster Streets.

Gateau:
4 oz. butter
4 oz. sugar
2 eggs, lightly beaten
2½ C. all-purpose flour
1½ tsp baking powder
½ tsp baking soda
½ tsp salt
1 tsp ground ginger
1 tsp cinnamon
¼ tsp nutmeg
¼ tsp ground clove
1 C. Steen's cane syrup
1 C. water
1 C. rum

Bruleed Meringue:
¼ C. sugar
¼ C. water
½ C. corn syrup
½ C. sugar
4 large egg whites

Gateau:
1. Cream butter and sugar until light and smooth.
2. Add beaten eggs slowly until combined.
3. Scrape sides with spatula and mix quickly.
4. Combine all dry ingredients in a separate bowl.
5. Combine water and rum in a saucepan and bring to a boil.
6. Pour over cane syrup in anther bowl.
7. Alternately add dry and wet ingredients to egg/sugar/butter mixture, mixing in between additions, and ending with wet ingredients.
8. Bake at 350°F until it springs back.
9. Serve with meringue.

Bruleed Meringue:
1. Whip egg whites on medium low until foamy; add one half cup of sugar slowly, turn mixer up to high and whip until stiff.
2. While the whites whip; combine one-fourth cup sugar and water and bring to a boil.
3. Add one-half cup corn syrup and bring to "soft ball" stage. This is 240°F or when the bubbles become large and pop slowly without browning on the edge.
4. Slowly drizzle syrup into the whipping egg whites and continue mixing on high until the bowl is cool to the touch.
5. When everything is ready to serve: spoon meringue on to cake and pass a blowtorch over it. If you don't own a blowtorch then put it in the oven on broil for a few minutes, until it resembles a roasted marshmallow.

Patois
6078 Laurel Street

"Dessert is probably the most important stage of the meal, since it will be the last thing your guests remember before they pass out all over the table."
William Powell

Monsoon

This neighborhood bar is consistently voted "Best Place to Get a Burger" in Gambit Weekly and Zagat as well as Citysearch, and if the line of hungry patrons is any indication, the word is out. Burgers and baked potatoes, stiff drinks and signature cocktails, proves this restaurant on Esplanade lives up to the hype. Open daily for lunch and dinner.

2 oz. 151 proof rum
2 oz. 80 proof rum
1 oz. Hawaiian Punch
concentrate
2 oz. orange juice
2 oz. pineapple juice
2 oz. Lemon Joy
(sour mix)

1. Mix together.

2. Pour over ice.

Port Of Call
838 Esplanade Avenue

"You can find your way across this country using burger joints the way a navigator uses stars...."
Charles Kuralt

Gravlax – House Cured Salmon with Dill, Akavit and Caraway

Ralph's on the Park is another of the famed Ralph Brennan Family of restaurants. Nestled amid the live oaks near City Park, Ralph's on the Park serves globally inspired interpretations of local cuisine influenced by the eccentricity, diversity and traditions for which New Orleans is known. Housed in an 1860 home, Ralph's is the perfect place for lunch, dinner or Sunday brunch.

3½ lb. salmon filet; skin-on
½ oz, (1 C.) fresh dill, leaves picked, reserve stems
4 oz. kosher salt
4 oz. sugar
1 Tbsp. fresh ground black pepper
½ tsp. curing salt
1½ oz. akvavit or 1½ oz. of gin with 1 Tbsp crushed caraway

1. Remove any pin bones and excess fat from salmon filet.
2. Lay reserved dill stems in a deep metal baking pan with high sides.
3. Mix together the salt, sugar, pepper and curing salt.
4. Moisten salmon filet with akvavit and sprinkle each side with fresh dill leaves.
5. Coat liberally each side of salmon with salt mixture.
6. Lay salmon in hotel pan upon the dill stems.
7. Cover salmon filet with a piece of parchment paper and another same size hotel pan.
8. Weight with two and one-half pounds (large cans of tomato etc.).
9. Place in refrigerator.
10. Turn salmon filet daily for four days.
11. Test texture and oil content of salmon filet before serving.
12. To serve, very quickly rinse filet, and wipe off excess brine.
13. Slice paper thin, on a bias.
14. Serve two and one-half ounce per serving with a Danish mustard sauce, and marinated cucumbers.

Ralph's on the Park
900 City Park Avenue

"As all cooks know, ingredients of the moment are the best guides."
Frances Mayes

201

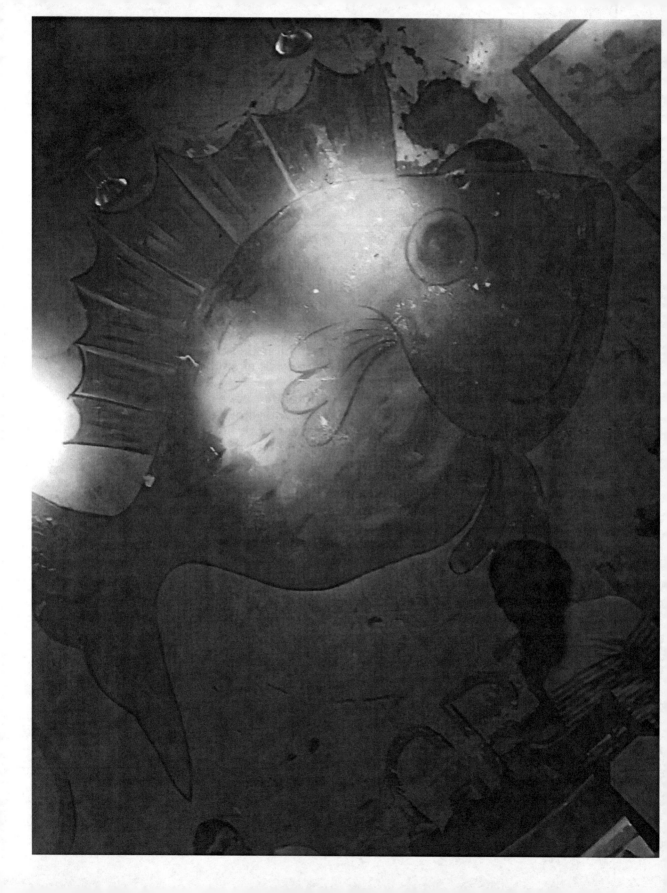

Sweet Potato Catfish with Andouille Cream Drizzle

Signature Taste of NEW ORLEANS

Red Fish Grill
115 Bourbon Street

Catfish:
1 (8 or 9-oz.) catfish filet, trimmed as needed
¼ tsp salt
1 tsp Creole seasoning
4 oz. Sweet Potato Crust
1 oz. clarified butter
3 oz. fresh spinach, cleaned
pinch Creole seasoning
pinch salt
pinch pepper
1½ oz. Andouille Cream Drizzle
chopped green onions

Sweet Potato Crust:
1½ lb. roasted sweet potato flesh
½ C. mayonnaise
¼ tsp salt
dash black pepper
2 Tbsp bread crumbs
⅜ tsp Creole seasoning

Andouille Cream Drizzle:
½ lb. andouille sausage, diced
1½ oz. vegetable oil
2 Tbsp Creole seasoning
2 Tbsp honey
1 qt. heavy (whipping) cream
3 oz. bourbon
3 Tbsp blond roux
salt, to taste
pepper, to taste

Sweet Potato Crust:
1. Roast (or bake) sweet potatoes.
2. Peel and place the sweet potato flesh and remaining ingredients in mixer.
3. Beat to incorporate.

Catfish:
1. Sprinkle the catfish with salt and Creole seasoning.
2. Spread the sweet potato crust on top of the fish.
3. In a hot skillet, add the clarified butter, then the fish, crust side up, to brown quickly.
4. Remove fish carefully and place in another pan, with a little of melted butter, if desired.
5. Bake in hot oven, 450°F, eight to twelve minutes, depending on thickness of filet. Do not turn fish. Don't over bake.
6. When fish is cooked, crust should be nicely browned.
7. Sauté spinach in clarified butter or margarine and season with Creole seasoning, salt and pepper.
8. Drain spinach and put in center of plate.
9. Place catfish on top, allowing the spinach to be seen on either side of the fish.
10. Drizzle the Andouille Cream Drizzle sauce around the fish and spinach.
11. Garnish the fish with chopped green onions.

Andouille Cream Drizzle:
1. Sauté andouille in oil until lightly browned.
2. Add Creole seasoning.
3. Deglaze pan - add the bourbon, scraping pan, tip the pan and pour off the bourbon and juices, leaving the grease to pour off and discard.
4. Return juices to pan and cook to reduce sauce slightly, watching carefully and stirring often.
5. Add honey and cream.
6. Add roux and let simmer until flour taste is gone.
7. Salt and pepper to taste.

"The best number for a dinner party is two – myself and a dam' good headwaiter."
Nubar Gulbenkian

Bread and Butter Pudding

New Orleans' crown jewel, The Ritz-Carlton combines all of the elegance of a classic hotel with modern amenities right on the edge of the French Quarter. Known for its Southern hospitality, The Ritz-Carlton New Orleans features a 25,000 square-foot spa, signature restaurant, stylish lounge and ample meeting space. This unique take on the traditional bread pudding will treat your guests to dessert, Ritz-Carlton style.

The Ritz Carlton, New Orleans
921 Canal Street

20 slices white bread, crust removed
1½ sticks unsalted butter, softened
10 large eggs
1 qt. whole milk
1 tsp. cinnamon, ground
1 vanilla bean, split and scraped
1 C. plus 2 Tbsp granulated sugar
¼ tsp salt
1 C. raisins
⅛ C. powdered sugar

1. Butter the inside of ten oven-safe individual serving dishes.
2. Butter bread slices and cut diagonally into quarters.
3. In a medium saucepan, scald milk, vanilla bean seeds, sugar, salt and cinnamon.
4. In a large bowl, whisk eggs and slowly pour hot milk over eggs, continuously whisking. Pour mixture through strainer to remove any lumps.
5. Arrange eight triangles of bread (two slices) in each of the ten oven-safe dishes and sprinkle one-half ounce of raisins over top.
6. Pour liquid over each dish evenly, about one cup, and allow to stand for about thirty minutes.
7. Bake in a water bath in oven at 325°F for twenty minutes.
8. After pudding is baked, pull out of oven and dust with a thin layer of powdered sugar.
9. Place under a broiler for about forty-five seconds, until the edges of the bread turn golden brown.
10. Serve immediately with vanilla sauce.

"A good meal makes a man feel more charitable toward the whole world than any sermon."
Arthur Pendenys

Shrimp and Mirliton Dressing

This locally owned, family oriented business provides New Orleans shoppers with all the convenience of a large impersonal chain store with the friendliness of a corner grocery. With convenient locations throughout the city, Robért Fresh Market has fresh made sushi, an extensive deli with prepared selections, locally grown produce, gourmet cheeses, wine, spirits and a gourmet bakery. During Mardi Gras season Robért Fresh Market is the place to get your king cake.

5 lb. mirliton, cut into 1" slices	**1.** Remove seeds and cut mirlitons into 1-inch slices.
1 lb. (70/90) shrimp, peeled and deveined	**2.** Boil mirlitons until tender.
2 C. onion, diced	
1 C. celery, diced	**3.** Drain water from mirliton pot.
1/3 C. red bell pepper, diced	
1/3 C. green bell pepper, diced	**4.** Mash mirlitons in pot.
1/3 C. yellow bell pepper, diced	**5.** Sauté shrimp and vegetables in skillet on high heat.
1 Tbsp thyme, dry	
1 Tbsp basil, dry	**6.** Add vegetables to pot with mirlitons.
2 C. seafood stock	**7.** Add herbs and seafood base and simmer for ten minutes.
10 oz. dry bread-crumbs	
1/4 lb. butter	**8.** Fold breadcrumbs into pot and remove from heat.

Robért Fresh Market
Various Locations

"No cook should be without garlic, parsley, onion and celery. I have listed them in the order of absolute necessity."
Angelo Pellegrini

Oyster Dressing

A Louisiana institution since 1960, Rouses grocery stores are conveniently located throughout the New Orleans area. Run by the second generation of the Rouse family, Rouses is the largest independent grocer in Louisiana. Offering shoppers full-service deli, meals to go, Cajun specialties, party trays and bakeries as well as wine and spirits, floral departments and even post offices in select locations, Rouses is many shoppers one-stop supermarket.

Signature Tastes of NEW ORLEANS

Rouses Supermarket
Various Locations

Cornbread:
1 C. self rising cornmeal
½ C. self-rising flour
¾ C. buttermilk
3 eggs
2 Tbsp vegetable oil

Dressing:
4 C. of Italian seasoned croutons
Cornbread
1 sleeve saltine crackers
1¾ C. chopped celery
1 large onion, chopped
8 Tbsp butter
2 C. vegetable stock
1 tsp salt
½ tsp freshly ground black pepper
1 tsp dried sage
1 Tbsp poultry seasoning
5 eggs, beaten
2 pt. or 1 qt. oysters, drained

Cornbread:
1. Preheat oven to 350°F.
2. Combine all ingredients and pour into a greased, shallow baking dish.
3. Bake for approximately twenty to twenty-five minutes.
4. Remove from oven and let cool.

Dressing:
1. Add croutons to cornbread and crackers.
2. Mix together and set aside.
3. Sauté chopped celery and onion in butter until transparent, approximately five to ten minutes.
4. Pour over cornbread mixture.
5. Add stock, mix well and add salt, pepper, sage and poultry season.
6. Add beaten eggs and mix well.
7. Add oysters and mix. Pour into a greased pan.
8. Bake for about forty-five minutes.

"There are four unbroken rules when it comes to Thanksgiving: There must be turkey and dressing, cranberries, mashed potatoes and pumpkin pie."
John Hadamuscin

Slow Braised, Wine Infused Boneless Beef Short Rib Roast with Honey Roasted Potatoes

Signature Tastes of NEW ORLEANS

2 to 4 lb. boneless beef short rib roast
kosher salt, to taste
fresh ground black pepper, to taste
2 yellow onions, diced
1 C. diced carrots
1 C. diced celery
½ C. balsamic vinegar
1 qt. beef stock or broth
8 garlic cloves, peeled
4 bay leaves
4 C. cabernet sauvignon
4 large russet potatoes, baked and cooled, cut in ½" slices
2 C. salad oil
2 Tbsp salt
1 tsp black pepper
3 Tbsp butter
2 oz. honey
4 C. prepared stone ground grits
4 oz. heavy cream
1 Tbsp truffle oil
1 Tbsp kosher salt
1 tsp fresh ground black pepper

1. Season the short rib top and bottom with kosher salt and pepper to taste.
2. Preheat grill. Place short ribs on the grill and watch carefully for flare-ups. Brown well on top and bottom. Remove short ribs from grill.
3. In the bottom of a cast iron pan or casserole dish place diced onions, garlic, carrots, celery and bay leaves.
4. Place short rib roast over onion mixture and top with liquid ingredients. Add salt and pepper if desired. Top pan with lid or aluminum foil.
5. Roast in a pre-heated 250°F oven for four to five hours until ribs are fork tender.
6. Remove from dish and strain remaining juice through a colander, reserving juice. Discard vegetables.
7. In a heavy saucepan, simmer pan juices over medium low heat until liquid is reduced to half its volume. Serve as an accompaniment with rib roast.
8. In a glass bowl place sliced onions and top with buttermilk and seasoning. Allow onions to sit.
9. In a large sauté pan, heat salad oil. Fry potato slices until they are brown on top and bottom, and remove from heat. Allow to drain on a paper towel.
10. In a small saucepan melt butter. Add honey and seasoning and allow to mix.
11. Lay potatoes on a cookie sheet and brush with butter mixture.
12. Roast in the oven at 350°F for eight to ten minutes. Serve with short rib roast.

Royal Sonesta Hotel New Orleans
300 Bourbon Street

"The South excelled in two things which the French deem essential to civilization: a code of manners and a native cuisine."
John Peale Bishop

Pumpkin Bread Pudding Pancakes

Ruby Slipper Cafe has expanded to two locations, one in Mid-City and another downtown and the warm and friendly atmosphere translates to both. Serving local products, committed to composting and recycling, as well as excellent, inventive cuisine make the Ruby Slipper the family's favorite locals' restaurant. Daily special pancakes include Crème Brulee, S'mores, Peanut Butter and Banana, as well as these luscious gems.

Pumpkin Bread Pudding Pancakes:

1 C. pancake mix (plus required egg and/or oil according to package directions, plus double the milk required by package directions)
2 tsp vanilla extract
⅛ tsp nutmeg
½ C. pumpkin puree
½ C. day-old french bread, cut into 1-inch cubes

Whiskey Sauce:

½ C. whiskey (of your choice)
½ C. heavy cream
1 Tbsp brown sugar
1½ Tbsp butter, softened
¼ tsp cornstarch
pinch salt

Pumpkin Bread Pudding Pancakes:

1. Mix the pancake batter according to package directions, using double the milk, and then add vanilla, nutmeg and pumpkin puree and mix until all ingredients are incorporated.
2. Add the French bread, and ensure it is well-coated with the batter.
3. Allow to stand fifteen minutes so that the bread absorbs the batter.
4. While pancakes are standing, heat the griddle to 375°F and prepare the Whiskey Sauce.
5. Lightly grease the griddle, then ladle one-third cup pancake batter onto the griddle for each pancake. Flip using spatula once bubbles form in the pancake and cook an additional one to two minutes.
6. Place pancakes on plate and spoon whiskey sauce on top.
7. You may want to double the whiskey sauce recipe if you like a lot of sauce.

Whiskey Sauce:

1. Heat sauté pan over medium high heat, add whiskey and flambé to burn off the alcohol.
2. Once flame goes out, lower heat to medium, whisk in heavy cream, and heat to just below boiling.
3. Add brown sugar and salt and continue to whisk until sugar dissolves.
4. Add cornstarch and continue to whisk, allowing the sauce to thicken.
5. Finish by adding softened butter, whisking slightly until blended.
6. Remove from heat.

Ruby Slipper Cafe
Two Locations

"It takes some skill to spoil a breakfast – even the English can't do it."
John Kenneth Galbraith
Street

Generally regarded as the world's first mixed drink, the Sazerac, first contained Sazerac de Forge et Fils brand of cognac as its prime ingredient. This drink contained bitters that were also made in New Orleans by Antoine Amedie Peychaud, a local druggist. The Sazerac House (formerly the Merchants Exchange) was the first to serve the drink. Around 1870 the primary ingredient changed from cognac to rye whiskey. After absinthe was banned in the United States in 1912, various anise-flavored spirits replaced it, especially Herbsaint, also from New Orleans.

¼ C. sugar
6 Tbsp Sazerac rye whiskey
6 dashes Peychaud's bitters
4 dashes Angostura bitters
2 tsp Herbsaint
2 thin strips lemon zest

1. Chill two rocks glasses or old-fashioned glasses in the freezer.
2. Meanwhile, make simple syrup by putting sugar and one-fourth cup water into a small saucepan.
3. Cover and boil over high heat, gently swirling pan over heat occasionally, until sugar dissolves, about two minutes.
4. Transfer simple syrup to a small bowl and set aside to let cool completely.
5. Fill a cocktail shaker with ice cubes.
6. Add Sazerac, Peychaud's and Angostura bitters, and two tablespoons of the simple syrup (save remaining syrup for another use) and shake well.
7. Swirl one teaspoon of the Herbsaint in each glass, coating insides with a thin film, and discard excess.
8. Strain Sazerac into glasses and garnish each with a strip of lemon zest.

123 Baronne Street (The Roosevelt New Orleans)

The Sazerac Bar

"Once, during Prohibition, I was forced to live for days on nothing but food and water."
W. C. Fields

Breau Bridge Benedict

Conveniently located on historic Jackson Square, Stanley serves up classic New Orleans comfort food in their provincial yet elegant dining room. Breakfast is served all day, but Stanley also serves brunch and luncheon sandwiches. House-made ice cream and the Stanley Burger are can't miss choices at this inventive restaurant. Travel and Leisure said they have "America's Best Pancakes" and we tend to agree.

2 eggs
2 pork boudin patties
1 tsp clarified butter
2 slices French baguette, sliced cross-wise 2-inches thick
1 slice American cheese
1 oz. smoked ham, diced
2 oz. hollandaise sauce
chopped scallion greens

1. Bring water to boil in a saucepan, then lower the heat.
2. Handling one egg at a time, crack the egg into a small cup and then gently drop into the water. Use a spoon to nudge the egg white closer to its yolk. Turn off the heat and let it sit for four minutes until the egg whites are cooked.
3. In the meantime, put the boudin patties in a preheated, non-stick sauté pan with the clarified butter over medium heat.
4. When the patties are golden brown, flip over and cook the other side.
5. Toast the bread and then transfer to a sheet pan.
6. Place the boudin patties atop the bread, add a cheese slice, and top with the diced ham.
7. Put in a broiler for about three minutes or until the cheese starts to melt. Remove from the broiler, place the poached eggs on top, and ladle on the hollandaise sauce.
8. Sprinkle with scallions.

Stanley
547 Saint Ann Street

"There's no better season for pancakes than springtime, when the sugar maple is running and fresh syrup is made."
John Hadamuscin

Spinach and Grape Salad with Blue Cheese Vinaigrette

Now with four and seven course tasting menus, Stella! in the French Quarter, serves globally inspired flavors with New Orleans palates in mind. Chef Boswell brings his international and multi-state culinary experience to New Orleans via a stint with Chicago's Chef Grant Achatz, Chef Charlie Trotter and Chef Jonathan Benno of New York City's Per Se restaurant, among others. Winner of numerous awards and mentions, Stella! is open nightly.

Salad:
1¼ C. small spinach leaves or other fresh greens (rinsed and dried)
2 Tbsp extra-virgin olive oil
salt, to taste
pepper, to taste
20 red California seedless grapes
20 green California seedless grapes
2 Tbsp toasted half walnuts, crumbled slightly

Blue Cheese Vinaigrette:
8 oz. blue cheese
⅓ C. vegetable oil
½ C. red wine vinegar
¼ C. sour cream
salt, to taste
pepper, to taste

1. Blend vinaigrette ingredients in a blender until smooth and form a loose paste.

2. Place walnuts on a baking sheet and toast for four minutes at 350°F.

3. Gently crumble walnuts after they have cooled.

4. Gently toss the spinach leaves in extra-virgin olive oil, salt, and pepper.

5. For a special presentation spread the vinaigrette dressing (about 1/3 cup) on the bottom of the plate and arrange the grapes in a decorative pattern on top. The grapes can be left whole at Stella!, they cut the ends off of each grape so they are a uniform size and can be stood up on end in a checkerboard or mosaic pattern. The grapes are then garnished with the toasted walnuts and baby spinach leaves or other fresh greens.

1032 Chartres Street

Stella!

"The fight is never about grapes or lettuce. It is always about people."
Cesar Chavez

Candy Cane Truffles

Signature Tastes of NEW ORLEANS

A sweet boutique on Magazine Street, Sucré offers your sweet tooth some-thing extra. Homemade French macaroons, some with New Orleans themed flavors, hand dipped chocolates, handmade seasonal marshmallows, toffees and crunches, candied nuts and other sweet treats are the perfect gift to take home to the dog sitter or house sitter. Pastry chef Tariq Hanna and founder Joel Dondis have teamed up to provide New Orleans with the perfect sweet satisfaction.

2 C. dark chocolate (65% or more)
1 ⅓ C. heavy cream
½ C. crushed candy canes
½ stick butter (room temperature)
1 tsp vanilla extract
1 C. cocoa powder
½ C. finely crushed candy cane

1. Combine heavy cream and candy canes in a non-reactive pot and boil until all candy cane is dissolved.

2. Pour over chocolate and stir until smooth.

3. Add butter and vanilla and stir until blended.

4. Place plastic wrap directly on ganache and refrigerate until firm.

5. Scoop quarter sized balls of ganache and roll in cocoa powder and finely crushed candy cane mix until well coated.

6. Best served at room temperature.

Sucré
3025 Magazine Street

"I've spent half a century jousting with the demons of flesh and chocolate."
Isabel Allendale

Bananas Foster French Toast

Offering New Orleans' freshest and finest breakfast and lunch, Surrey's has been a neighborhood staple since 2001. Fresh-squeezed organic juices, wheatgrass shots and seasonal choices combine with local seafood, sausages and produce to create healthy, yet tasty dishes. House-made bagels and biscuits, pancakes, egg dishes and French toast await hungry, health conscious diners. Both locations are open daily.

Bananas Foster Mix:
3 bananas
4 C. dark brown sugar
8 oz. cream cheese, softened
2 Tbsp vanilla extract

French Toast Batter:
2 eggs
1 tsp vanilla extract
2 Tbsp sugar
1 C. half-and-half

Bananas Foster Sauce:
1 lb. butter
3 oz. dark brown sugar
½ Tbsp vanilla extract
¼ C. rum
2 oz. heavy cream
loaf French bread, cut in 4 pieces
powdered sugar, for garnish

Bananas Foster Mix:
1. Add all ingredients except one banana and thoroughly mix with the handheld blender until it is well combined and uniform.

French Toast Batter:
1. Whip eggs and sugar with a whisk.
2. Add vanilla and whisk until sugar has completely dissolved.
3. Continue to whisk while adding the half-and-half.

Bananas Foster Sauce:
1. In a hot pot over medium heat, melt butter and brown sugar with the vanilla. Wait until butter is completely melted.
2. Remove pan from the heat, add the rum and ignite with a long kitchen match.
3. When the flames die down, add the cream immediately and whisk vigorously until sauce is completely smooth.

Assembly:
1. Heat some oil in a large sauté pan.
2. Stuff four quarters of hinged French bread, with the reserved sliced banana, and top with the cream cheese stuffing.
3. Slice the four portions of filled bread into four diagonal pieces, dip into the batter and pan-fry on all sides until golden brown.
4. Pour the warm rum sauce on a plate.
5. Place the golden pieces of toast on top and garnish with powered sugar.

"Yes, we have no bananas. We have no bananas today."
Frank Silver and Irving Cohen

Collard Green, Black-eyed Pea, Bacon and Bourbon Soup

A unique and sophisticated restaurant concept in the historic French Quarter, Sylvain was opened in the Chartres' Street carriage house of famed landmark developer, Don Andres Almonster y Roxas. The menu expertly blends both the past and the future with elevated bistro classics, a storied wine program and a cocktail selection that leans on the classics while embracing the resurgence of the cocktail culture.

6 bacon slices, chopped
2 yellow onions, sliced
4 cloves garlic, minced
1 bunch collards, roughly chopped and rinsed well
2 oz. white wine
2 bay leaves
½ tsp chili flakes
3 qt. pork stock or chicken stock
2 oz. good Kentucky bourbon
1½ C. cooked black-eyed peas
1 tsp. fresh thyme leaves
salt, to taste
pepper to taste

1. Slowly render bacon until crisp.

2. Add onions and sauté until tender (about five minutes).

3. Add garlic and sweat until fragrant.

4. Add collards to the pot to wilt.

5. Deglaze pot with white wine and add the bay leaves and chili flakes.

6. Add stock and bourbon and bring to a simmer.

7. Continue to cook until the collards are tender (approximately twenty minutes) then add black-eyed peas and thyme.

8. Adjust to taste with salt and pepper.

Sylvain
625 Chartres Street

"What was paradise, but a garden full of vegetables and herbs and pleasure? Nothing there but delights."
William Lawson

The first Taqueria Corona opened on Magazine Street in 1983 with two wire-spool tables and ten stools at the bar. Today this family-owned and operated taste of Mexico has three locations, run by Roberto Méndez and his three brothers. Méndez uses all fresh ingredients, hand cut produce and trimmed lean meats to make his authentic dishes. Try one of the eight top-shelf Tequilas or a house margarita.

1-2 large bundles of green onions (about 30 onions)
3 tsp vegetable oil
3 tsp lime juice
½ tsp salt
1 tsp crushed garlic
juice of 1 lemon
1 pickled jalapeño (halved)
1 tsp jalapeño pepper juice (from can)

1. Line a shallow sheet pan with one piece of aluminum foil.

2. Toss all the ingredients together and fold the ends of the foil together to create a sealed foil envelope so that the juice cannot escape and that steam will build up around the onions.

3. Broil on high for thirty-five minutes.

4. Unwrap the foil pocket exposing the onions. (Be careful when opening the foil as hot steam will escape.)

5. Add one pat of butter to the onions.

6. Broil open for five to ten minutes more until a desired char is achieved.

7. Sprinkle with additional salt and garnish with lime.

Taqueria Corona
Various Locations

"The man that isn't jolly after drinking is just a driveling idiot, to my thinking."
Euripides

Shrimp Remoulade

Tujague's is the second oldest restaurant in New Orleans, opened in 1856, and still serving Creole cuisine in the French Quarter, near the French Market. Produce is selected from the French Market and other local ingredients combine to create an authentic New Orleans experience. Two dishes have been a part of the prixe fixe menu since its inception, shrimp remoulade and beef brisket boiled with aromatic vegetables and served with Creole horseradish sauce.

1 C. ketchup 2 Tbsp horseradish 2 Tbsp yellow mustard 2 Tbsp Worcestershire sauce dash Tabasco 4 hard boiled eggs, chopped 2 raw eggs, beaten 1 gal. water 1 package crab boil 3 Tbsp salt 36 large raw shrimp shredded lettuce	**1.** Mix the first seven ingredients in a glass bowl. **2.** Chill in the refrigerator four hours. **3.** In a large pot, bring the water, crab boil and salt to a full boil. Add shrimp. When the water returns to the boil, turn off the heat and let the shrimp sit for five minutes to absorb the seasonings. **4.** Drain the shrimp, cool and then peel them. **5.** Place six shrimp on a plate lined with shredded lettuce and top with four tablespoons of the sauce. Repeat five more times.

Tujague's
823 Decatur Street

"Food, it appeared could be important. It could be an event. It had secrets."
Anthony Bourdain

Fried Green Tomatoes
with Shrimp Remoulade

Upperline serves Louisiana food, serious wine and Creole hospitality in their Uptown neighborhood, just a short streetcar ride from the French Quarter. The restaurant houses more than four hundred art objects and memorabilia each with New Orleans associations, that have been collected over the years by owner JoAnn Clevenger. Each year Upperline host a series of special occasion dinners including a Lousiana Réveillon Dinner during the December holiday season.

Signature Tastes of NEW ORLEANS

Upperline Restaurant
1413 Upperline Street

Tomatoes:
1 egg, large
1 C. buttermilk
1 C. yellow cornmeal
½ tsp salt, plus as needed
¼ tsp freshly ground pepper, or as needed
8 green tomato slices, 1½-inch thick
6 Tbsp vegetable oil
24 shrimp, medium, peeled, cooked and chilled
1 C. Remoulade Sauce, chilled
8 oz. mixed greens

Remoulade Sauce:
½ C. Creole mustard
2 Tbsp ketchup
1 tsp Worcestershire sauce
2 tsp prepared horseradish
1 tsp garlic clove, medium, finely chopped
1 tsp lemon juice, fresh
1½ tsp paprika
¼ tsp freshly ground white pepper
⅛ tsp fresh finely ground black pepper
⅛ tsp cayenne pepper
salt, as needed
½ C. olive oil
¼ C. celery ribs with leaves, finely chopped
1½ tsp. parsley, finely chopped
2 Tbsp yellow onion, grated
1 Tbsp green onion top, finely chopped
hot sauce (optional) as needed

Tomatoes:
1. Whisk together egg and buttermilk in a medium bowl. Reserve.
2. Combine cornmeal, salt, and pepper in a shallow dish. Reserve.
3. Dip tomato slices in egg mixture, then coat with seasoned cornmeal.
4. Heat oil in a large sauté pan over medium heat.
5. Place tomato slices in pan in a single layer, and cook until golden brown on bottom, approximately six minutes, turning once.
6. Plate two tomato slices; top each slice with three shrimp.
7. Sauce each slice with one and one-half tablespoons Remoulade Sauce.
8. Garnish with greens and serve.

Remoulade Sauce:
1. In a small mixing bowl, combine first ten ingredients.
2. Add salt as needed.
3. Whisk in olive oil until emulsified.
4. Add celery, parsley and onions; stir well.
5. Add hot sauce.
6. Cover and reserve, refrigerated.

"I don't care what anybody says: Nothing is better than a tomato you grow. There's something about it that's different than a tomato you can buy. It's a great thing."
Tom Vilsack

Frenchmen Scallops

This restaurant has expanded from its Frenchmen Street location to the West End, giving yet another neighborhood their authentic Japanese dining experience. Serving lunch and dinner it is possible to eat in the Japanese style dining room or at their large sushi bar. Try the sake or Japanese beer selections at their full bar. Reasonable prices, wide selection of sushi and friendly service can be found at either location.

6 jumbo sea scallops
2 Tbsp minced garlic
⅓ stick butter
1 Tbsp Hondasbi
(Japanese fish stock)
cornstarch
3 Tbsp vegetable oil

1. Coat scallops in cornstarch.

2. Heat oil in frying pan, and then add scallops when oil is hot.

3. Pan fry scallops for one minute on each side or until golden brown.

4. Add garlic and butter.

5. When butter has completely melted, add Hondashi.

6. Sauté in pan for one minute.

7. Remove scallops from frying pan with tongs, and then pour sauce from pan onto scallops.

Wasabi Sushi and Asian Grill
Various Locations

"Nothing ever tasted better than a cold beer on a beautiful afternoon with nothing to look forward to but more of the same."
Hugh Hood

Willie Mae's Gumbo

2 qt. water
8 Tbsp vegetable oil
1 bell pepper, chopped
3 onions, large, chopped
15 to 20 garlic cloves, chopped
2 scallion bunch, chopped
4 to 5 celery ribs, chopped
3 lb. okra, chopped
1 lb. Creole hot sausage (or spicy sausage of your choice), sliced into 1-inch rounds
2 lb. smoked sausage, sliced into 1-inch rounds
2 lb. ham, chopped into 1-inch pieces
2 Tbsp flour
2 (12 oz. can) tomato sauce
2 (12 oz. can) tomatoes, peeled
3 to 4 lb. shrimp, peeled and deveined
6 crabs, cleaned and halved
½ bunch flat-leaf parsley, chopped
salt, to taste
freshly ground pepper, to taste
steamed rice, as needed

1. Heat water in a large soup pot over medium heat.
2. Heat six tablespoons oil in large skillet over medium-high heat.
3. Fry peppers, onions, green onions, garlic and celery in batches until soft.
4. As each batch is cooked, put vegetables in pot of water.
5. Reduce skillet heat to medium and fry okra until it is largely dry, about thirty minutes.
6. Put okra in soup pot.
7. Fry sausages and ham, in batches if necessary, until grease has been rendered.
8. Put meat in soup pot and discard grease.
9. Heat remaining oil in skillet.
10. When hot, whisk in flour and cook roux until tan but not too dark.
11. Add roux to soup pot.
12. Add tomato sauce to soup pot.
13. Chop peeled tomatoes and add to pot.
14. Bring gumbo to a boil, then reduce heat to medium and simmer for 1½ hours.
15. Add shrimp, crabs and parsley and season with salt and pepper.
16. Serve over steamed rice. (Consistency of complete dish should be more like chicken and rice soup than rice and gravy.)

Willie Mae's Scotch House
2401 Saint Ann Street

"I come from a family where gravy is considered a beverage."
Erma Bombeck

Ye Olde College Inn

RESTAURANT & BAR

Since 1933

Uptown ⚜ New Orleans

(504)866-3683

www.collegeinn1933.com

Oyster Omelet

Signature Tastes of NEW ORLEANS

This New Orleans landmark in Uptown began as The Pig Stand, a chain restaurant from Texas. When prohibition ended and the lease payments were pending, the Rufin family decided to try a restaurant on their own. The College Inn, later adding Ye Olde to differentiate it from the competition, had air conditioning, car-hop service and still stands as a testament to one thing that doesn't change, good food and good service. Now owned by another family, the Blanchers, Ye Olde College Inn Restaurant and Bar still prides itself on good food and service.

8 oysters
1 oz. mushrooms, chopped
1 oz. green onion, chopped
1 oz. Italian parsley, chopped
4 oz. white wine
2 oz. slurry
3 eggs, beaten
2 drops yellow food coloring (optional)
2 dashes hot red pepper sauce
4 oz. water

1. In a 10-inch skillet, poach the oysters, green onions, mushrooms and parsley until the oysters are cooked through.

2. Add the white wine and let simmer for thirty seconds. Add the hot sauce and slurry and bring to a boil quickly to thicken.

3. Add food coloring (if using) to eggs and pour the eggs into a large skillet or onto a fiat grill, sliding the eggs around until they are completely cooked.

4. Once cooked, pour half of the oyster filling inside the eggs and fold in all the edges.

5. Pour the remaining filling on top of the omelet.

"Food has always meant more than feeding. Food is bonding, sacrament, joy. A quotidian public delight."
Sallie Tisdale

Steven W. Siler is a firefighter-cum-chef serving in
Bellingham, Washington. Long marinated in the epi-
curean heritage of the Deep South, Steven has spent
over 20 years (dear God has it been that long?!) in the
much-vaulted restaurant industry from BOH to FOH to
chef. In addition, he has served as an editor and contributing writer for several food publications. When not
trying to shove food down his fellow firefighters' gul-
lets, he enjoys sailing and sampling the finest of scotches
and wines, and has an irrational love affair with opera.
He swears one day he will relive the above picture on
the Gulf Coast with a good Will.

Paula Garriott is an award-winning writer who has covered such diverse topics as politics, crime and entertain-
ment in her mostly journalism career. She has served as
communications director for several organizations and has
also worked in the fundraising arena.

The daughter of a butcher, she has been refining her palate
since childhood and loves to cook. An avid cookbook col-
lector herself, she currently has more than 100 vintage,
specialty and regional cookbooks. This is her second cookbook. Signature Tastes of Las Vegas was released in spring
of 2012.

Paula first came to New Orleans in 2004 and lived there
during Hurricane Katrina. Although she moved to Las
Vegas in 2006, she gets back to the Crescent City several
times a year, is a Mystic Krewe of Nyx sister, doesn't miss a mardi gras and she
knows what it means to miss New Orleans, enough that she is working to move
back to her adopted home.

SIGNATURE TASTES   **HIDDEN EATS**   **TABLE FACTS**   **BYGONE ERAS**   **ART OF CULINARY DIPLOMACY**   **VARSITY**   **SUBLIME NECTAR**

CPSIA information can be obtained at www.ICGtesting.com
Printed in the USA
LVOW11s0443051113

360027LV00008B/212/P